D1167431

This book is funny, honest, and tac[...] speaking the truth in love, and the pow... of our words from a biblical standpoint. It is the perfect book for our social media driven world. My friend Karen Ehman says everything that needs to be said about how to "Keep It Shut."

LYSA TERKEURST, *New York Times* bestselling author of *The Best Yes* and president of Proverbs 31 Ministries

Keep It Shut offers hope for all of us who struggle with controlling our tongues. Karen's honest and compassionate advice teaches us how to weigh our words and think before we speak. I've put Karen's wise suggestions to the test and am already noticing an improvement: less talking, better listening! Helpful, practical, biblical.

LIZ CURTIS HIGGS, bestselling author of *The Girl's Still Got It*

Words are the most powerful weapons we have. They can be a sharp sword or a soothing salve, both having the ability to change someone's path in an instant. I wish every one of my social-media followers would read this book along with me.

CANDACE CAMERON BURE, actor, producer, New York Times bestselling author, *Dancing with the Stars* Season 18 finalist

Our words have the power to build up or to destroy. It's no wonder that the Bible compares the tongue to both forest fires and swords. Karen Ehman's book offers solid biblical counsel for those who want their words to be vessels of grace and healing.

JIM DALY, president, Focus on the Family

Karen Ehman's creative way of sharing stories to help get a point across and her passion for Scripture made it easy for me to accept the truth that there is wisdom in knowing what to say, how to say it, and when to say nothing at all.

JENNIFER SMITH, blogger at The Unveiled Wife, author of *Wife after God* and *The Unveiled Wife*

Our words matter! *Keep It Shut* will be my go-to guide for years to come. Karen Ehman covers it all—from gossip, flattery, and lying to words that heal and give courage. She is spot-on scripturally, profoundly practical, and humorous! This book is a life changer!

COURTNEY JOSEPH, author and blogger at
WomenLivingWell.org and GoodMorningGirls.org

At some point in our lives, I am betting that every one of us has thought, "Why, did I just say that?" My friend Karen understands. In *Keep It Shut*, we learn the power our words have and when to use it effectively to minimize regrets and maximize results.

JENNIFER ROTHSCHILD, author of *Lessons I Learned in the
Dark, Self Talk, Soul Talk*, and *God Is Just Not Fair: Finding
Hope When Life Doesn't Make Sense*, founder of Fresh
Grounded Faith events and womensministry.net

Understanding the often subtle difference between words that help and words that harm can sometimes be a challenge. Karen Ehman's humor and heart shine through as she gives women the tools to navigate through the potential minefield of words in our daily lives.

RUTH SOUKUP, founder of LivingWellSpendingLess.com
and author of *Living Well, Spending Less:
12 Secrets of the Good Life*

The tongue is a mighty sword, which can be used as a weapon of warfare or an instrument of healing and peace. In *Keep it Shut*, Karen Ehman wisely reminds us to be conscious of this powerful force and to use it wisely in wonderful ways.

DARLENE SCHACHT, author of *Messy Beautiful Love:
Hope and Redemption for Real-Life Marriages*

If I had a dollar for every time my mouth got me into trouble, I could pay to have it surgically shut. What a relief to discover I'm not alone in my struggle! Karen Ehman dares to share the ups and downs of her own wrestling match with words. And with the precision and care, she gives us the tools we need to cut out the destructive habits and create healthy new ones.

MICHELE CUSHATT, author of *Undone: A Story of Making
Peace with an Unexpected Life*; emcee of Women of Faith

Once a week (or more than once a day) I regret something I said. I'm so grateful Karen Ehman has come to my rescue with her own honest struggles, regrets, and hard-fought wisdom packed with a humorous punch in her new book, *Keep It Shut*. This is a girlfriend's guide to no-regret-living I'll be hanging onto for a long while!

RENEE SWOPE, bestselling author of *A Confident Heart* book and devotional, Proverbs 31 Ministries' Radio cohost, *Everyday Life with Lysa & Renee*

What a wonderfully relevant and significant book! Karen has packed this book with timeless, life-changing wisdom. Every woman needs to buy this book and read it at least once a year! Highly recommend!

SALLY CLARKSON, author of *Own Your Life and Desperate: Hope for the Mom who needs to Breathe*, popular speaker, and blogger at Sallyclarkson.com

I love Karen's writing! It's like you're sitting down having a conversation with a girlfriend. Open these pages and be encouraged, challenged, and equipped to use your tongue to bring life to your relationships!

JILL SAVAGE, CEO of Hearts at Home, author of *No More Perfect Moms*

As a graduate of the Speak-First-Think-Later-School of Communication, I can relate to every word written in *Keep It Shut*. But instead of telling me to go into a corner and just stop talking, Karen comes alongside and shows us how we can powerfully use our words for God and others' good.

KATHI LIPP, author of *The Husband Project* and *The Cure for the Perfect Life*

In *Keep It Shut* Karen Ehman embarks on a much-needed conversation. She keeps it real, fun, and relatable. A must-read in a world where opinions swirl and their effects are deeply felt.

MICHELLE MCKINNEY HAMMOND, author of *Getting Smart About Life, Love and Men*

Everyone with a mouth like mine needs this book! Karen Ehman has a gift. She shares a message we need to hear in a way that is helpful, not condemning. I'm thankful for how Karen encourages women to lead like Jesus from head to toe.

COURTNEY DEFEO, author of In *This House, We Will Giggle*
and creator of ABC Scripture Cards

In typical Karen fashion, she does an excellent job of weaving great Bible content with authentic personal stories, her down-home humor and grace, and thought-provoking, reflective questions. *Keep It Shut* has my highest recommendation!

CINDY BULLTEMA, Speak Up Conference speaker
and author of *Red Hot Faith*

Karen's wisdom and truth reminds me that just because we're able to say it, doesn't necessarily mean it's beneficial; and *how* we choose to say things is just as important as choosing *when* to say them.

SUMMER SALDANA, lifestyle and beauty blogger at
summersaldana.com

Whether you consider yourself a "talker" or not, *Keep It Shut* will challenge to consider what words you let fly out of your mouth as you dive deep to consider their source.

CINDY BEALL, speaker and author of
Healing Your Marriage When Trust Is Broken

Keep It Shut is a powerful challenge for those of us who tend to speak first, think later. Karen has invited us to join her on the quest to use our words wisely (even when that means not using words at all!).

TERI LYNNE UNDERWOOD, blogger
www.TeriLynneUnderwood.com

I have believed in Karen's potential since she was a teenager. I have seen the Lord turn her weaknesses into strengths for the benefit of others, including how she uses her words. This book is so needed!

PATRICIA BEASLEY, Karen's high school pastor's wife
and mentor since 1980

KEEP IT
SHUT

ALSO BY KAREN EHMAN

Let. It. Go.: How to Stop Running the Show and Start Walking in Faith

Let. It. Go. Study Guide with DVD

KEEP IT SHUT

SHUT

WHAT TO SAY, HOW TO SAY IT, AND WHEN TO SAY NOTHING AT ALL

KAREN EHMAN

ZONDERVAN

Keep It Shut
Copyright © 2015 by Karen Ehman

Requests for information should be addressed to:
Zondervan, 3900 *Sparks Dr. SE, Grand Rapids, Michigan* 49546

ISBN 978-0-310-33965-6 (ebook)

Library of Congress Cataloging-in-Publication Data

Ehman, Karen, 1964-
    Keep it shut : what to say, how to say it, and when to say nothing at all /
Karen Ehman.— 1st [edition].
      pages cm
    ISBN 978-0-310-33964-9 (softcover)
    1. Oral communication—Religious aspects—Christianity. I. Title.
BV4597.53.C64E36 2015
241'.672—dc23   2014040224

Published in association with The Fedd Agency, P.O. Box 341973, Austin, TX 78734.

Cover design: Dual Identity
Cover illustration: iStockphoto®
Interior design: Katherine Lloyd

First printing November 2014 / Printed in the United States of America

19 20 PC/LSCH 25 24 23 22 21

She used her words for good and for God.
I miss her contagious smile and cheerful attitude.
Every. Single. Day.

Dedicated to my sister-in-law,
Thais Ehman VanGinhoven,
February 3, 1955 – October 29, 2014

CONTENTS

1

FROM SPARKS TO RAGING FIRE

The Awful Power of the Tongue

Death and life are in the power of the tongue,
and those who love it will eat its fruits.

PROVERBS 18:21 ESV

I sat alone at a corner table in the sterile, gray, middle-school lunch-room fiddling with the peas and carrots on my mustard-colored plastic lunch tray. I wasn't sitting at the usual table near the front of the lunchroom. That privilege was reserved only for those in the popular group at my midwestern school in the late 1970s.

Oh, how different things had been just a week prior! I was privileged to hang out at the "cool table" then, occupying one of its sought-after metal and Formica spaces. But that was before "it" happened: my banishment from the popular group, which resulted in my need to sit at a normal table like the rest of my eighth-grade class.

I could feel the clique of teens staring at me even though I never looked up from my tray. I can only imagine the things they were saying about me. How could I have let this happen?

How could I go from being one of the popular kids to now dreading school so much, especially lunchtime when the hierarchy of middle-school culture was on full display there in the lunchroom. Why?

Because of my words.

My words had brought me to this place. Just a week earlier I had been with a group of the "in" crowd of boys. I was the sports reporter for the school newspaper. We were laughing and discussing our basketball team's latest triumph over our crosstown rival. But soon the conversation turned to what many middle schoolers talk about: what boys liked what girls, and vice versa. The wintertime dance was coming up, and so naturally the topic rose to the top of our talk.

One of the boys was considering taking a friend of mine whom I'll call Janet. I knew Janet really liked this boy, but I also knew a secret about her, a secret that, although nothing serious or scandalous, was embarrassing nonetheless. You see, at the last dance in the fall she had snuck a kiss with another boy in our class under the bleachers when no chaperones were looking. That boy was one of my good friends, and he confided in me just what his opinion was of the stolen kiss: he thought that she kissed like a fish!

Now I should not have taken this juicy piece of information and wielded it against my friend, but I loved to get attention from the boys in my class (and I secretly had a crush on the boy who wanted to take Janet), and so I let the words tumble out. "Hmm … You might want to think that one through. You see, Bill Warner said he thinks Janet kisses like a fish."

At that the entire group of boys burst into roaring laughter. I assumed that this meant Janet would get no invitation to the winter dance and the top secret info I leaked would never be divulged to her. But I was wrong. Instead of this information deterring any boys from asking her to the dance, the one who had been considering taking her instead proceeded to tell her what I said. And to ask her to the dance anyway.

To say that she was upset would be an understatement. She was livid! She gathered all of the popular girls around, and together they shook their heads in disbelief, their Farrah Fawcett–style bangs swaying in the air, as they expressed their horror that a girlfriend could do such a thing to another sister. It didn't take long for the mob of middle schoolers to make a choice and then take action. They completely banned me from the popular group. No longer could I sit at their table, occupy a space next to them on the bleachers during a sporting event, or even sit near them in any of our classes. For the first time in my nine years of going to public school, I absolutely dreaded going. I had a stomachache every morning riding the bus to school. I was lonely walking through the halls between class periods. And once home, the phone never rang with one of the girls calling, wanting to chat.

Trying to find a new group of kids to hang out with halfway through the school year in eighth grade can be rather difficult. Cliques have formed. Friendships have been forged. And it just didn't seem there was any room for a "cool kids" reject like me. My only relief came from a group of three girls who took me in and allowed me to sit with them in the lunchroom. But the weekends were torturous and lonely.

No longer did I get invited home after school to hang out for a few hours with one of my former friends. There were no more invitations to roller-skating parties. Or Friday night sleepovers. Not even an invitation to hang out at the mall, grab a soda and an afternoon matinee, and just enjoy being thirteen.

The remainder of the year was hard, and I was so thankful to see summer vacation. Thankfully, the next year when I entered high school we would be joining with another middle school to form our freshman class. I hoped and prayed that this would mean I could find a new group of friends and begin to enjoy being a teenager again.

Sometimes I still think about that lonely eighth-grade year and how my choice to repeat something that was said brought about such a horrible time in my life. Now, what I said was not a lie. Bill Warner had said that she kissed like a fish. But my decision to repeat those words was a poor one. Especially when he later denied he ever said it! (And of course that was way before text messaging, so I couldn't save his words as a screenshot for proof later.)

My little middle-school drama taught me one important lesson:

Our words are powerful, and they have consequences.

Whether it is a string of words screamed out in anger during the height of a marital spat, or a politician who chooses to lie in order to win votes, or even just a middle schooler trying to impress a group of boys. Our words are powerful, and our words have consequences.

It Only Takes a Spark . . .

"It only takes a spark to get a fire going . . ." So started the popular campground song I sang growing up in my local youth group. Each night as we sat staring at the flickering flames of the campfire, someone would start to sing that popular chorus. One by one, each of us would join in, proclaiming the power of sparks to get a fire going, until all of the voices were singing in unity, making loud praise with our voices.

Our words are like sparks. They may start small, but they can ignite a wildfire of destruction and devastation. The author of the book of James was the first to make the analogy: "Likewise, the tongue is a small part of the body, but it makes great boasts. Consider what a great forest is set on fire by a small spark. The tongue also is a fire, a world of evil among the parts of the body. It corrupts the whole body, sets the whole course of one's life on fire, and is itself set on fire by hell" (James 3:5–6).

Yes, what starts as a little spark can soon gain momentum and become a booming blaze.

In the early summer of 2013, I flew to Colorado Springs for a radio show taping. I have been to the Springs several times in the past and always look forward to my visits there. Although the plane ride is a long one, the descent into Colorado is always breathtaking. My heart leaps as I view the mountains and the lush green grass and the natural rock formations.

This landing, however, was different. Just a few days prior, a horrible fire had broken out, and now the Black Forest Fire, as it was called, raged all around. Off in the distance I could see smoke. At other places I could see the blackened, charred remains of what had once been green foliage.

A friend had lost her home. Others on Facebook asked for prayers for relatives and friends of theirs who also were affected by the flames. When it was all over, 486 homes were destroyed, and two people died. The Black Forest Fire was considered the most devastating fire in the history of the state, and the images I saw and the social media about it were terrifying. All in all, over 14,000 acres were burned, and the damage was estimated at over $85 million.

Just how did this disaster start? Record-setting heat had been in the region and a red flag warning from the National Weather Service had been issued. In the early afternoon hours of June 11, a man reported a tiny structure on fire, so small that he could capture the flames on his cell phone camera. However, the record heat coupled with the blowing winds soon fanned the flames, and the fire spread to over 100 acres. And then it spread to 1,000 — and on and on and on.

How fitting that James should use fire as an analogy for how our words can quickly spread, causing untold damage. No wonder the Bible cautions us to be very careful with our words. They are fiery indeed!

Corrupt and Untamable

The passage in James also talks about how the tongue can corrupt our whole body. I myself know very well from the times I have wished I could take back my words; often my whole body is affected. My mind races with regret. My heart pounds. My stomach churns and becomes tied up in knots as I fret and stress over what now might happen. My fingers fidget, and I can't seem to concentrate. Sometimes my feet pace as I ponder what I possibly can do now to get myself out of the royal mess I now find myself in.

If we read a little farther in James, we find that the tongue cannot be tamed (James 3:7–8). Every creature, reptile, bird, or animal can be tamed, but not the tongue. Imagine a colossal circus full of every kind of creature: dancing bears, prancing horses — even a ferocious looking feline or two performing tricks or jumping through hoops when their trainers give the signal. But way off in one corner stands a booth with a closed curtain and a sign that reads: "The Utterly Untamable." Then, at a very strategic time during the spectacular show the ringmaster hushes the audience in order to display this beast that will not bend. When he throws open the concealing curtain, sitting behind it is a woman on a cell phone, chatting away!

With our tongues we curse men and women who are made in God's likeness and then, at other times, we praise God. Out of our mouths flow both praising and cursing. But, says the New Testament writer, this should not be! James tells us that a spring cannot suddenly shoot out both sweet and bitter water. Neither can a fig tree produce olives or a grapevine decide to grow a whole mess of figs instead of grapes. You can't get salt water from a freshwater spring (James 3:9–12). Lesson? We should not have both righteous and evil words coming from our tongues.

Misusing My Mouth

Often my mom used to say to us kids, whether we were leaving to go to school for the day or headed off to a weekend social gathering, "Be sure your sins will find you out." There was no shortage of sins to choose from growing up as a midwestern teenager in the seventies and eighties. However, I chose to stay away from the cigarettes and booze and drugs. My problem was not with what went *into* my mouth. My problem was what came *out*.

My words, sometimes even my lack of words, have caused me much pain over the years. It hasn't always been that I have gossiped or lied. Sometimes I just talk too much. Or I repeated the words of others, which I should not have. Other times I have tried to say the right thing, but it came out the wrong way. Or I have said the right thing but in the presence of the wrong people or at the wrong time. There was just no shortage to the ways I could misuse my mouth.

A survey through the Bible reveals that God places great importance on the way we use our speech. In fact, the words *tongue, talk, speak, words, mouth,* and *silence* are used over 3,500 times in the Bible. The pages of Scripture are full of people just like you and me. Some of them serve as a great example of how we should use our words to build up, encourage, and speak for truth. However, there are others who seem to be the poster children for just how *not* to use our mouths. They gossiped, whined, lied, hurled sharp and angry words, or just said the wrong thing at the wrong time. They tempted and urged others to sin. They told half-truths that really were whole lies. Or maybe they said the right thing but at the wrong time or to the wrong person. This resulted in many outcomes: from hurt feelings to wounded relationships to even all-out wars between nations.

It really is the same today. Over the course of the last thirty years of my adult life, I have seen words bring about dire situations. I have also seen them bring about much good. Truly, death and life are in the power of the tongue. The key is knowing how to use our speech properly.

Psychiatrist Louann Brizendine states in *The Female Brain*, "Men use about seven thousand words per day. Women use about twenty thousand."* (I do know of a few cases where I'm sure this is reversed, where the husband is a yacker while the wife is pretty quiet!) Although Brizendine's figures are still much debated, just using the numbers on the lower range of both of these estimates means that in the course of a year, women speak about 7.3 million words and men utter about 2.5 million words. All of these words flying off of our lips give ample opportunity for mistakes, fumbles, and foibles. It also gives lots of room for intentionally harmful words. But we must also think of the flip side! How many words of love and care and encouragement can we speak over the course of a year? The choice really is up to us, since we are the ones who control our flapping jaws.

The Origin of Our Words

The Bible says that life and death are in the power of the tongue (Proverbs 18:21). Before the words can get onto our tongue and

---

* Louann Brizendine, *The Female Brain* (New York: Morgan Road Books, 2006), 4.

spill out of our mouths, don't they begin somewhere else first? Yes, our words may emit from our lips, but they originate in our minds and hearts before they find their way up to our mouths and then to the ears of others. If we really want to learn to control our tongues, knowing what to say, when to say it, and when to say nothing at all, we need to drill down deeper. We need to delve into our hearts and minds to discover the origin of our words, both the life-giving ones and the ones that deal the deathblows.

The apostle Luke says, "A good man brings good things out of the good stored up in his heart, and an evil man brings evil things out of the evil stored up in his heart. For the mouth speaks what the heart is full of" (Luke 6:45).

The mouth speaks what the heart has stored.

You see, my words don't just tumble out of my mouth randomly or by mistake. They are purposeful and intentional, having originated first in my heart. So if we have a mouth problem, in actuality what we really have is a mind and heart issue. Even in the case of my words gone wrong in middle school, it wasn't just that I spoke the wrong words. My mind entertained a wrong fact that turned into a wrong motive. My heart was intent on evil. I just couldn't bear the thought of my latest crush and Janet going to the dance together. So an idea first formed in my mind. Then it trickled its way down into my heart where a root took hold. Then, out of the abundance of my heart, the words bubbled up and spilled out of my lips, thereby causing pain, in this case not only for Janet, but mostly for me.

The truth is, words are never accidental. To be sure, there are times we utter careless words, but even then those words are first formed in our minds, filtered to our hearts, and then given permission to come out of our lips. So in our quest to use our words in ways that are good and honor God, we must first consider the heart and mind from which they come.

Care of the Heart and Mind

Every two or three years, my husband and I go to a center that does (for a very reasonable price) an entire battery of medical tests. His mother paid for us to go the first time about ten years ago just after his father suffered a stroke. His grandmother had also suffered a stroke, and so my mother-in-law was very concerned that if there were any early warning signals of Todd or me possibly being susceptible to stroke, then she wanted us to know.

Thankfully, each year these tests have shown that not only are our bones good and strong, but our hearts are in excellent condition too. If we had trouble brewing under the surface and were not having these tests administered, we might perhaps one day wake up with chest pain or a heart attack or maybe even a stroke. But because we are being careful to monitor things underneath, we can be alerted if something starts to go wrong before we notice it.

Long before our words go wrong, our hearts are the place in which they fester and brew. We must take very careful care of our hearts and their condition so that the words that come forth will be pleasant and sweet instead of hurtful and bitter. But just how do we do this?

Over thirty years of being a Christian, I have learned some very important things about the connection between my words and my heart. How I use my words, whether for good or for evil, can often, although not always, be traced back to the quality time I am (or am not) spending with the Lord each day, how intentional I am about investing in my relationship with him, and whether or not I am taking steps to become more like his Son, Jesus Christ.

This caring for the heart — the source of my words — isn't some kind of spiritual hocus-pocus where I simply open up my

Bible and the latest bestselling devotional book and read a few words each morning. It requires being attentive to God's still, small voice throughout the day. Yes, I should be reading my Bible daily and spending time in prayer asking God to help me temper my words and my resulting actions. But the most important thing is responding to the Holy Spirit's tap on my heart when he whispers to me, urging me not to say something I'm about to blurt out or nudging me to speak up when I instead want to remain silent. Caring for my heart in those moments means asking the Holy Spirit to give me wisdom — to keep silent when that is best, or to give me the right words to say when I just can't seem to find them. Perhaps a friend has lost a loved one or is suffering because of some choices they or a close family member made. Or maybe I just need a little help creatively wording something for my children to really get a point across, so instead of just hearing Mom lecture again they really listen to the truth behind my words.

So yes, by all means grab a good devotional book. Crack open your Bible. Hit your knees in prayer. But do it all with an attitude of openness that continues throughout the day. Be attentive to the Holy Spirit's whispers to you — keep silent if that is the Spirit's leading. Or open your mouth and allow the words he is whispering and urging you to say to come out in your own sweet little voice. It isn't easy. It takes effort. It is always easier to ramble or hurl thoughtless words than it is to pause and then choose our words carefully.

Are you willing to try — really try? If you've struggled with words like I have, you may have some mixed feelings in response to this question. You really do want to try, but you also remember times you've "really tried" and failed. If that's the case, allow me to whisper a little encouragement to that word-weary heart of yours. Believe me when I say that if it is possible for someone like me to run her words through the grid of God's holiness, it is more than possible for you to do the same. One step at a time, prayer by prayer and word by word, we really can temper our talking so we have fewer words floating out there that we wish we could take back. It *is* possible — for me, and for you.

The Journey Begins . . .

Are you ready for the journey? A quest to learn to say what we should, when we should, and to know when to say nothing at all? Today, you can hit the Restart button on the way you use your speech. (Or perhaps click the Force-Quit command, shutting it down altogether?) Maybe words you utter to a family member. The language you use with your coworkers. How you talk to your neighbor. Even the words that tap out from your fingertips and onto the computer screen online.

Consider this your better-than-a-middle-school-sleepover invitation to hang out with me as we learn together to temper the untamable tongue, thus keeping the whole body in check. For starters, in the days ahead I invite you to begin each day with this simple prayer:

Father, I face another day in which I will be called upon to use my words wisely and well. May they encourage those who listen. May they speak truth but also be said in love. May I pause before I pounce. May I be bold enough to speak when I would rather run away. Lord, I give my mouth to you today. May what comes forth be sweet and not bitter. May the journey each word takes from my mind to my heart to my lips be guided by your hand. May what comes out be life-giving rather than causing death. May my words make you proud and bring you glory. In Jesus' name, Amen.

2

SQUABBLES, SPATS, AND SUCH

How to Communicate with Family, Friends, and Other Necessary People

Hatred stirs up conflict,
but love covers over all wrongs.
Wisdom is found on the lips of the discerning.

PROVERBS 10:12 – 13

They are an odd, but pretty pair, the two candlesticks we have perched on the antique dresser in our master bedroom. While both are crafted from solid brass with similar round and sturdy bases, the shafts of each candlestick couldn't be less alike.

One is straight and streamlined, not at all fancy, just functional, with tall lines, direct and strong. The second is designed with a touch of flair; two equidistant strands of brass whirl and swirl side by side in a "look at me" manner as they ascend to the top of the shaft that holds the candle in place.

I found each candlestick at a different yard sale, both in the same month. While their styles aren't the same, somehow this eclectic pair is an interesting match. And more importantly, they are a constant visual reminder to my husband and me, providing a tangible picture of our marriage.

My husband is the first candlestick. No frills. Straight-forward. All about function.

I am the second one. Crazy. Winding. All over the map. Completely about fun.

While we both are "forged from brass" in that we are followers of Christ with the same spiritual foundation, pair our opposite-end-of-the-spectrum personalities together and disaster could ensue. In fact, we often joke that if in our courting college days we would have been able to send our profiles to an online matchmaking website, instead of pairing us up with each other, the computer screen would have blinked a bright warning. DO NOT DATE! TOTALLY NOT COMPATIBLE!

Pictures of Perfection?

So often in this day and age of online dating, larger-than-life romantic movies, and spectacular stories of love and romance making their way all over the Internet, it is easy for us to get a picture of marriage that blinks of perfection. And it isn't just with marriage. So many smiling, well-dressed, and seemingly well-behaved families also parade before our eyes on social media day after day. New moms post a parade of glowing baby and toddler photos on Instagram. Teens on Facebook tag their siblings in a post saying how "awesome" and "amazing" they are on the track team or in the school musical. Delighted parents praise their children (and rightly so) for their newly earned honor of "Student of the Month" or "Captain of the Soccer Team." And every picture-perfect post makes our own family relationships seem to fall so short by comparison.

Yet, in all of these snapshots of flawlessness, there is a missing component. We do not see how these family members are interacting with one another. Sure, they may praise each other publicly, but they don't display their squabbles and spats for all the world to see. (At least not most of the time!)

Interacting day after day with our loved ones is not always easy. (Can I get an amen?) Parents and children have conflicts over many things both large and small. Even couples who are head over heels in love with each other are bound to clash at times. Squabbles, spats, and such are an inevitable hazard of life lived in close quarters.

Beyond the normal male/female differences between married couples, any two personalities in close proximity will inevitably cause friction, conflict, and sometimes (mostly from me) snapping and harsh words. In fact, no matter if it is in marriage, parenting, or in a work or friendship situation, we're bound to experience frustration, anger, and at times, wounded feelings. People who are not wired as we are, who don't think like we do, and who make decisions and carry out actions we would never dream of, are going to rub us the wrong way. That's a fact.

Usually, in dealing with a frustrating non-family member, we manage to keep our composure, tame the tongue, and not do or say anything that we might later regret. I've often wondered why I can usually (but not always) keep my cool with people who are not members of my own family. Let's say the cashier at the grocery store makes a mistake in counting out my change. It's an honest and innocent blunder. She didn't mean to do it. Now I don't go all ballistic on her, raising my voice or even speaking in a subtle but snarky tone to let her know that someone who has a job as a cashier should surely know how to correctly make change. Nope. I usually smile and chuckle and say that it's really no problem. I certainly don't make her feel stupid, nor do I use my words, eye rolling, or shoulder-shrugging sighs to imply such.

With people outside my family, I may want to keep up a good image and not have them think ill of me, so I choose my words wisely, making sure to not err on the snarky side. Even if it is someone I will never see again, I am careful to make sure my words are pleasant and inviting and don't cause the person to think I am unkind or rude.

When it comes to my friends I am usually pretty careful with how I word things, making sure not to upset or offend them. Even when a friend says something I think is foolish or behaves in a way I think may be unwise, I usually manage to hold my tongue. Perhaps if this person is an extremely close friend and asks my opinion about something, I may speak the truth in a straightforward manner. But for the most part, I try to keep my mouth shut in order to keep the peace and avoid offenses or awkwardness.

But with members of my own family I can be so different! If someone in my inner circle makes a mistake, I've been known to subtly or even overtly make backhanded comments about it. Or if one of my children is assigned a household task and doesn't do it correctly, I don't really think about my words as I interact with them. I simply let them spill out. And what tumbles out isn't always pretty. Why is this so?

Perhaps because I am related to these people and share the same last name or bloodline, I sometimes feel I can cross the line of decency when it comes to my words. I don't have to fear that these people are going to decide not to hang out with me or to spread the word that I am an awful person. They are family, and my relationship with them will not end just because of a few cross words between us. Can you relate?

"Familiarity breeds contempt," so the old saying goes. And there certainly isn't any group of people we are more familiar with than those who live under the same roof. This familiarity can tempt us to drop our standards when it comes to how we use our words. No longer are we careful not to offend. In fact, sometimes we offend on purpose!

With our children or spouse, sometimes we open the flood-gates and spew out all sorts of cutting comments, nasty words, fly-ing criticisms, and awful accusations. We can even use silence as a weapon. When we give someone the cold shoulder, we may hold in our words, but we're spewing out our feelings all the same. My husband and I call this misuse of words (or withholding of words) "throwing flesh balls." At that point, we are not "walk[ing] by the Spirit" but "gratify[ing] the desires of the flesh" (Galatians 5:16).

My flesh just likes to be gratified sometimes, and noth-ing gratifies it more than a good ol', all-out verbal assault on my "thinks-and-acts-so-different-from-me" husband. He tends instead to use his cold-shoulder silence to make his feelings known and dig the knife in, twisting it for effect. But is this what God intends for people who call themselves his followers? Are our words weapons, and even our silence part of the arsenal?

For decades, TV shows have built whole seasons around household squabbles. Remember *Everybody Loves Raymond*? Ray and the Barone family had conflicts galore. And even back in the good ol' days, the wholesome Brady kids had spats, and the salt-of-the-earth Waltons got into a scuffle or two. Why, even on *Little House on the Prairie*, Laura and Mary Ingalls fought at times. And the *Bonanza* boys often found themselves in an all-out fistfight right there on the Ponderosa! (Little Joe, my per-sonal favorite, often got the brunt of it.) Of course, these domes-tic disputes were usually solved within thirty to sixty minutes, ending with a smiling brood enjoying each other in the last scene of the show. Yes, it isn't just recently or just on TV that families have hit rough spots in their relationships. The pattern goes back even further.

An Ancient Reality Show

The story of Joseph and his family has always fascinated me. The saga of this family in Genesis 37–50 plays out almost like an ancient reality show. And I am simply in awe of the ways that Joseph uses both his words and his silence for good. He did it when he interacted with his family members, and he did it when he interacted with those he encountered in the workplace. Let's take a little peek at the story now.

Joseph's father Jacob had a couple of wives and a boatload of kids. Even though I'm sure the popular self-help books of his day told him not to, he had a favorite child. This child was Joseph, who had been born to his wife Rachel. Jacob even had a nifty coat of numerous colors specifically crafted for Joseph, who must have paraded this prized piece from his papa in front of his brothers enough that it made them very jealous.

To make matters worse, Joseph was starting to have big, self-important dreams. When he awoke, he shared what he'd dreamt with his older brothers, even when his dreams suggested all of his siblings would one day bow down to him. While that is indeed what eventually happens, you can imagine that sharing all the details of these dreams didn't win Joseph any "Brother of the Year" awards from his siblings. Instead, they hated him all the more. In fact, his brothers could not even stand the sight of him. Whenever he came upon them out in the fields, they uttered under their breath, "Here comes that dreamer."

One day when his brothers had gone out to pasture their father's flock at Shechem, their dad sent Joseph to see how they were doing and then bring word back to him. After searching for a while and asking a man out in the field where he might find them, Joseph stumbled upon his brothers at Dothan. Instead of being excited to see their brother and extending the family high five and handshake, they decided to do away with him — murder their own flesh and blood. However, big brother Reuben spoke up and said, "Let's not take his life. Let's throw him into a pit instead." (He intended later to come back and rescue him and return him to their father.) And so into the dry cistern Joseph was tossed. (Another "Little Joe" picked on by his big brothers.)

Later, the boys pulled him out of the pit and came up with a different plan. They decided to turn a little profit on the whole shady deal by selling him to a group of Ishmaelite traders who were headed down to Egypt. Then they returned home and told their father that Joseph had been killed by wild animals, providing his once colorful but now blood-soaked garment as proof of the tragedy. Jacob was distraught beyond belief.

Joseph, once a favored son, was now a slave in the house of Potiphar. This man was a well-to-do official in the land of Egypt. He had a big house and nice things. He also had a very flirtatious wife who set her sights on the young and hunky Joe. I've always thought of her as the first desperate housewife. Although I've never watched that show, I think the housewives usually seduce the pool guy or some other unsuspecting (and inappropriate) male. And this is precisely how we see Mrs. Potiphar behaving.

When one day she finds Joseph all alone, Mrs. P. approaches him with a lusty request. "Come to bed with me!" Joseph, who fears God and wants to honor him even though he is now in a strange land, does not sin with his words. Instead, he plainly states the truth to his boss's wayward wife: "With me in charge ... my master does not concern himself with anything in the house; everything he owns he has entrusted to my care. No one is greater in this house than I am. My master has withheld nothing from me except you, because you are his wife. How then could I do such a wicked thing and sin against God?" (Genesis 39:8–9).

In using his words to answer this seductress, Joseph not only honors his boss but he also honors his God. He answers her in accordance with what is right, both as an employee and as someone who follows the one true God.

Joseph had a choice to make. He could have chosen to use his words for evil. He could have accepted her advances so as not to offend her and had an immoral relationship with her. Then he could have continued to use his words to cover up the deed, making sure his master never found out about it; and if confronted, he could have lied about the incident. But because Joseph chose to speak the truth from the beginning, he didn't have to continue to use deceitful words to cover up poor choices.

However, even good and true words have consequences. Mrs. Potiphar, who didn't consider her advances an immoral mess, engaged her lying tongue to spread the story that Joseph tried to rape her. Joseph was summarily thrown out — not into a dry cistern this time, but into the Pharaoh's prison.

Once behind bars, the plot only thickens. Joseph meets up with a couple of new characters. One is the chief cupbearer for Pharaoh and the second is his baker. When both men have dreams they can't understand, Joseph interprets for them. For one man it turns out grand — the cupbearer is released in three days and goes back to his old job. However, the baker doesn't get such a joyful interpretation. Instead, he is put to death after three days. Joseph asks the cupbearer to remember him when he goes back to serve Pharaoh. Unfortunately, the cupbearer is so excited to be bearing cups again, he plumb forgets about Joseph.

Later, however, when Pharaoh himself is tormented by dreams that include fat cows and skinny cows, the cupbearer suddenly remembers the clever guy in prison who could make sense of bizarre dreams. Joseph is summoned. The dreams are interpreted. Pharaoh discovers through Joseph's words that there will be seven years of plenty and then seven years of famine. Joseph's advice? Pharaoh must find a discerning, wise man and set him over all of the affairs of Egypt, saving up food during the years of abundance to make sure they have plenty to go around in the years of famine. Well, who better to be in charge of such a plan than Joseph? He soon enters the service of the king with a whole administration under his command. He marries and has two sons just before the famine arrives. Circumstances finally seem to be going his way.

Meanwhile, back in his hometown, Joseph's family is quickly running out of bread and milk (and probably figs and dates too). Upon learning that there is grain in Egypt, Jacob turns to his sons and says, "Why do you just keep looking at each other? ... I have heard that there is grain in Egypt. Go down there and buy some for us, so that we may live and not die" (Genesis 42:1 – 2).

So all the brothers minus the youngest, Benjamin, trek off to Egypt in search of a little grub. When they come before Joseph, he immediately recognizes them. They, however, haven't a clue who he is. By this time years have passed, his looks have changed, and he dresses and speaks as an Egyptian, not as one of them.

Joseph decides to help his brothers but not without testing them first. Over the course of time, they travel back and forth between Egypt and their homeland and eventually fetch Benjamin. When Joseph discerns that they are being honest with him and dealing properly, he finally reveals who he is. He sends all of the servants out of the room and weeps loudly as he reveals his true identity to his brothers. The first question on his lips is, "Is my father still living?"

The brothers are so terrified they can't respond. They're sure Joseph will kill them for their treachery. But instead of retaliating, Joseph assures his brothers they have nothing to worry about. They shouldn't even be angry with themselves for selling him into slavery, because Joseph is certain God sent him to Egypt ahead of his family to preserve their lives.

The entire brood is then reunited, and Jacob gets to see the son he presumed was dead. It seems like a happy ending to a fierce family feud. Joseph provides his family with land to settle in, and they begin to make a living once again. However, years later when their father dies, the band of brothers is afraid that Joseph has only been biding his time — faking forgiveness for the sake of their father — and now he's going to let them have it. After Jacob's funeral and burial, the brothers go to Joseph and plead, "We are your slaves!" They send a messenger to ask Joseph to please forgive their transgressions and all the suffering they caused.

He could have had them executed or enslaved, but instead, Joseph responds with compassion. "Don't be afraid," he says. "Am I in the place of God? You intended to harm me, but God intended it for good to accomplish what is now being done, the saving of many lives. So then, don't be afraid. I will provide for you and your children" (Genesis 50:19–21). And he continued to reassure them and speak kindly to them.

And then? Just like a classic episode of *Bonanza* ("Old, old East" rather than "Old West" style), well, they actually do live happily ever after.

Cues from Joseph

Just what can we learn from this tale of drama lifted right off the pages of the Old Testament? What cues can we take from Joseph about how we should — and should not — use our words when dealing with family, friends, and other necessary people in our lives?

First ...

1. Beware of Bragging — and the Impact Your Good News Could Have on Others

Although for most of Joseph's life we see him using words wisely and well, many biblical scholars suggest that the young Joseph had a problem with pride. When he relayed his high and mighty dreams to his siblings, it set them on edge. We don't know what Joseph's motives were, and we don't know the condition of his heart, but neither do we read that God instructed him to tell his brothers about his dreams. Still, we can learn something from the consequences of his words to his family.

Sometimes we may have a piece of information that is indeed true. However, relaying that bit of information to someone else may not always be the wisest course of action. Before we open our mouths, we need to think about not only to whom we're speaking but also what they may be dealing with at the time and how the news might impact them. Did you just find out you are expecting your third child? Fabulous! But if your sister-in-law, who is childless, recently suffered her second miscarriage, then it might be best to hold off on your news for a while — and then consider carefully how you will let her know. The primary principle is to check your heart and motives before sharing a success or celebration. Also be mindful that — even if your heart is in the right place — how and when you share your news just might put a pinch in another person's heart, especially if they are sorrowful over the very thing about which you are rejoicing.

2. Say What Honors God, Not What Other People Want to Hear

When Potiphar's wife was chasing Joseph around the mansion, he knew what she wanted to hear. He also knew that giving her the answer she wanted was the furthest from what God desired. Joseph could have gone along with her little plan and then kept it a secret from his boss, but he knew God was watching. And listening. He chose to speak words that honored God rather than to please the ears of the person in front of him.

Most of us aren't usually faced with someone wanting us to break the law or do something immoral and against Scripture. However, there are times when answering according to what we know another person wants to hear conflicts with what we know to be true in Scripture. One of the authors of Proverbs writes, "The heart of the righteous weighs its answers, but the mouth of the wicked gushes evil" (15:28). I certainly know there have been times in my life when my words just gushed out. I knew the answer I gave didn't please God. But I was so intent on pleasing the person standing in front of me (or on the other end of the phone) that I just started gushing. Unfortunately, what leaked out was wrong.

We must purpose to weigh our answers. Weighing fruit at the supermarket sometimes takes a few minutes of back-and-forth as we add and subtract to adjust the scales. But when we do the same with our words, mulling over our response before it tumbles off the tongue, we have a much greater probability that the fruit of our words will please God. And then? We can trust him with the consequences. If the other person doesn't like our answer, so be it. We must make it of greater importance to please the Lord.

3. Realize That Lies Are the Minuscule Snowflakes in a Monumental Snowball

Because Joseph was truthful, he had no need to lie to cover up for what he might have done. Nor did he have to tell even more lies to cover up the first one. Lies must be followed by other lies, and they soon become a giant, rolling snowball, wreaking havoc on everything in its path.

In middle school, I was a pitcher on the softball team. I simply loved to play and wanted to make sure my skills were at their best so I could don my colorful jersey and be chosen as the starting pitcher of the game. So, while my mom was busy at work one day, I went down into my basement to practice throwing pitches, using the middle cushion of the couch as home plate. (This wasn't fast-pitch softball, obviously.)

My little practice session went well, with most of the pitches landing squarely on the middle cushion of the big brown couch. However, one of them got away and sailed clear out our basement window, taking dozens of puzzle pieces of broken glass with it. Now I'd like to say that when my mom got home from work I told her what happened and offered my sincerest apologies. However, instead, I lied.

First I denied even knowing about it. Then I said it must have been my brother and his friends playing outside. However, when my smart — and sometimes smart-aleck — brother cleverly pointed out the fact that the glass was on the outside of the house rather than the inside, I knew I was sunk. The ball had to have been thrown from inside the basement out into the yard, not the other way around. And I was the only one inside the house that day. My string of untruths soon began to unravel. If only I had told the truth from the beginning, there would've been no need to continue twisting words in order to deceive. And my punishment would have been much less than the punishment I got for not only breaking the window, but also initiating a cover-up.

4. Give God Credit Where Credit Is Due

How easy it is to take credit for ourselves. But Joseph's example shows just how much he learned from the failures of his early, bragging days. Whenever others marveled at his ability to interpret dreams, he rapidly pointed out that it was God who did the interpreting. I wonder how many of us, when receiving compliments from a high government official, would be quick to give all the credit to God. How easy it would be to smile and say, "Oh, it's nothing really," rather than declare, "Oh no — it's all God. Not me. And he is really something!" Joseph knew where credit was due. God gave the talent. God gave the ability. God arranged the circumstances so he could use his talent and ability. And so it was God, and God alone, who should get any credit for the good things that resulted.

5. Watch Your Words in the Workplace

Beyond our immediate family members, perhaps the people we spend the most time with are our coworkers or colaborers in church, community, or school committees. We spend so much time with these people they are almost like family, so it's easy to let down our guard with what comes out of our mouth. But Joseph didn't shut the filter off when he was around his working buddies. Whether in service at his master's house or in the cold dark prison, he watched his words. He knew that how he behaved and what he said reflected on the God he served. This is something we must also keep in mind as we work alongside others who are watching, absorbing, and then determining just what our God is like.

6. Just Because You Have a Reason to Retaliate Does Not Mean You're Justified in Doing So

Oh boy, if there were ever anyone who had the right to retaliate, it was Joseph! Sure, we might have family squabbles or old wounds that just don't seem to heal. Perhaps a family member has offended us in the past and now there is a great chasm of silence between us. Maybe someone's words rubbed us the wrong way and now there is tension whenever we get together as a family. Got that coworker who said something bad about you in an email, and somehow it made its way to your desk? Or that other parent down at the PTA who you are just sure does not like you? Scenarios such as this sometimes tempt us to retaliate.

Maybe that retaliation isn't an all-out assault on the person. It could be something subtle. You might use facial expressions or silence to convey your disapproval when that person's name is brought up in a group setting. Maybe you are on a committee selecting a student for an award, and the child of the person who offended you just happens to be one of the kids up for it. Even though you think this child is probably most deserving of the award, you vote for someone else instead. And who knows what devious ways of retaliation our minds can concoct when it comes to our family members? I'll just let you fill in the blank there. And even if it's not from your own life, I suspect you certainly have seen this happen a time or two.

It challenges my heart in the greatest ways to think that Joseph did not retaliate. He had not just been talked about publicly in a negative way or given the cold shoulder by an extended family member — he was thrown away and left for dead! If he can forgive those who did such evil to him, then why, oh, why can't I step back from the urge to retaliate?

7. Don't Be God

Joseph went beyond just giving credit to God for the good things and talents in his life. Most importantly, he knew his position — and God's. When his brothers approached him after their father's death, begging for him not to retaliate, his answer was quick and clear: "Don't be afraid. Am I in the place of God?" (Genesis 50:19). Then he proceeded to turn a horrid family feud into a timeless tale of forgiveness. "You intended to harm me, but God intended it for good to accomplish what is now being done, the saving of many lives. So then, don't be afraid. I will provide for you and your children" (Genesis 50:20–21). Even though Joseph surely could have used his position of power to deliver a punishing blow to his brothers, he chose not to. He realized that in God's divine plan, the evil they intended had instead been transformed into fuel for the fire of good. Joseph didn't question God or complain. He didn't take it out on his brothers. He let God be God while he was content to simply be himself: a servant.

8. Do Be Nice

After Joseph announced to his brothers that he was not God, he "reassured them and spoke kindly to them" (Genesis 50:21). Talk about turning the other cheek! He not only reassured them of their safety, he spoke kind words, even going so far as to say he would provide for them and their children, which is exactly what he proceeded to do.

What a simple yet significant lesson — one we should all have learned way back in kindergarten.

Simply. Be. Nice.

Did a family member slight you and you are still stewing about it? The next time you're around them try this: Be nice.

Did the other soccer mom jockey for position on the snack committee, leaving you in the dust? The next time you encounter her on the sidelines, try this: Be nice.

Got a coworker you know who talks behind your back? Don't lower yourself to their level, adding to the workplace drama. Try this instead: Be nice.

Be nice.

Be nice.

BE. NICE.

Maybe this is what my mama meant when the eighth-grade

girls were all being mean to me and she told me to "Kill them with kindness." (Or "Knock them over with niceness" perhaps?)

Joseph's behavior not only inspires me, it reminds me of Jesus. My former pastor once showcased in a sermon sixty similarities between Joseph and Jesus. (I respectfully pointed out that he'd missed one. They both start with "J"!) So, when we try to emulate Joseph's godly behavior, we are also — in a sense — being like Christ.

For example, when we choose to speak words that honor God — rather than massaging our words into what we think someone wants to hear — we follow Joseph's example, but ultimately we mirror Christ. His words always pleased the Father even when some people didn't agree or understand.

When Jesus tells his disciples he will soon be going away, it wasn't what they wanted to hear (John 16:16–18). His companions did not understand (and I'm sure they didn't agree with the timing), but he knew his death on the cross was the Father's perfect plan, and so speaking these words pleased God. (And his death on that cross for the sins of the world opened the way to heaven for those of us who believe in him!)

What does it look like to speak words that honor God, rather than speaking what someone else wants to hear? It may mean speaking truthfully about our views on an issue even if we know the other person's views are polar opposite and they'd much prefer we agreed with them. (Insert "awkward tension in the air" here!) And our words — though not what the other person wants to hear — must always be delivered with gentleness, respect, and grace.

Most of us understand what it means to be gentle. And respect? We get that too. But what does it mean to speak with grace?

I'm so glad you asked.

Laced with Grace

The words *grace* and *gracious* are used 169 times in the Bible. Often the word *grace* is used to describe how God deals with us. How he lavishes us with this gift. But just what *is* grace?

In the Old Testament the Hebrew word used for grace is *chen*. Its meaning is tightly tethered to God granting a person favor, and it is often worded that so-and-so "found favor" in God's eyes. A central part of its meaning is that the person being spoken about pleased God immensely.

The New Testament uses the Greek word *charis* when talking about the concept of grace. The essence of this word is that we receive the unmerited favor of God. Over and over, Scripture affirms that grace is something freely given. There is no cost on our part. But there was a cost to Christ. We can only receive this saving grace by trusting in Jesus Christ as our Savior and staking our lives on the promise that his sacrifice on the cross paved a way for us to spend eternity in heaven with God.

When my husband first began his life with God, he was part of a Bible study called — appropriately — *Life with God*. The minister who taught the class gave the students a clever way to remember just what grace is: G.R.A.C.E. is **G**od's **R**iches **A**t **C**hrist's **E**xpense. The apostle Paul's words to the church at Ephesus affirm this description of grace: "For it is by grace you have been saved, through faith — and this is not from yourselves, it is the gift of God — not by works, so that no one can boast" (Ephesians 2:8–9).

When Scripture describes God as gracious, several times the words "compassionate" and "slow to anger" are also used. The psalmist sums up God's character with this amazing description: "But you, Lord, are a compassionate and gracious God, slow to anger, abounding in love and faithfulness" (Psalm 86:15).

God is patient. He doesn't fly off the handle in anger. His love never runs out. His faithfulness never takes a vacation day. And God's Son knew how to impart grace when he spoke while here on earth: "All spoke well of him and were amazed at the gracious words that came from his lips" (Luke 4:22).

Many verses in Scripture affirm that our speech should be gracious. When we choose to grant favor with our words or to lavish love on someone through our speech, we mirror Christ and his free gift of grace. "Let your conversation be always full of grace," writes the apostle Paul (Colossians 4:6). One wise author of Proverbs says, "Gracious words are pure in [God's] sight" (15:26), and "Gracious words promote instruction" (16:21).

What is the result of intentionally speaking graciously to our family, friends, and other necessary people? Of loving them without stopping? Of containing our anger when we speak and dealing with them in a patient and faithful way? When we choose to lace our words with grace, healing happens: "Gracious words are a honeycomb, sweet to the soul and healing to the bones" (Proverbs 16:24).

Yes, choosing grace will sometimes cost us. Spats and squabbles are oh-so-easy to fall into. We will have to resist the urge to lash out in anger. We might even have to bite down on our tongues. But better a bleeding tongue than a family member's wounded heart. We might have to choose to let go of the need to prove our point, choosing instead to do the right thing: to impart grace and deal with the other person in love and with utmost patience.

When we choose to do this — even though it can be extremely difficult — we model to those closest to us a picture of Christ loving his church. Fights are abandoned. Tempers cool off. Stress simmers down. Our gracious words wash over the other person with love and compassion. We find ourselves faithful to God.

When we lace our words with grace, healing happens.

Every day, we can choose to apply the truth and promise of these wise words: "Hatred stirs up conflict, but love covers over all wrongs. Wisdom is found on the lips of the discerning" (Proverbs 10:12–13). This snippet of Scripture provides direction for how to handle with grace the inevitable conflicts that arise when we react to those in our inner circles of life.

So, when a colleague or fellow committee member is bossy and condescending, we can refuse to add to the negative tone of the meeting. How? By resisting the temptation to bark back or respond with additional condescension. Instead, we can choose to speak honestly — with words that are direct — but that are also strategically tucked inside an envelope of grace.

When a family member's behavior threatens to knock the nice right out of us, we can pause. Recalculate. Punch in a different destination for the words now downloading from our brains onto our tongues. We can program them to first stop at gentleness, swing by to pick up respect, and finally — arrive with grace. Then our mouths can utter pleasant words rather than those that are caustic, cutting, and unkind.

Take the advice I sometimes have to give to myself: Don't say something permanently painful just because you are temporarily ticked off.

Will you join me today in choosing to stop stirring up strife when it comes to someone in your life who is oil while you are so water? Yes, even if that person is your spouse? Or your child? Or your in-law? Or the coworker in the cubicle next to you? Or the grumpy neighbor across the street?

God intentionally orchestrated the relationships in our lives. He knew who would share your last name — or your four walls. Who would occupy a seat in your car pool or dwell in the house right next door. It didn't surprise him who would wind up as your in-law or be the one to teach your kids.

All the humans you encounter throughout the course of the day are "on purpose" people. God plopped them into your life for a reason.

These souls — whether they are of the easy-to-love variety or the scratchy sandpaper kind — can be used by God to mold, reshape, and sometimes stretch our souls as he perpetually crafts us into creations who are becoming more and more like his Son.

Will we be perfect?

Nope. Never. (Not until heaven!)

Just like Joseph?

Maybe close.

But of this I'm certain: others can catch a quick glimpse of Jesus when they see us speak and act in ways that honor him and line up with God's Word.

Others are watching, sizing up how we behave. What will they see? Stirred-up strife — or lovingly covered offenses? Speech that incites spats and squabbles? Or speech that soothes and heals?

You choose. (Pssst.... The correct answer is "g." Grace.)

3

STOP FILLING THE GAP

Learning to Listen

Come, my children, listen to me;
I will teach you the fear of the LORD.

PSALM 34:11

My family calls me the gap filler. I'm not sure I'm too keen on that nickname, but I guess I earned it fair and square.

For as long as I can remember, I have loved to talk. My gift for gab was what my relatives commented on when I was little. My constant chatter entertained not only my neighborhood friends, but also their moms, who reported all the highlights to my mother. There's nothing cuter than a precocious little girl who has a winning way with words. However, once the little girl begins to grow up, her gift of gab can become a detriment rather than a delight. And I got my first taste of the detriment side of the equation in elementary school.

As a young girl, I simply loved going to school. Even the awful scratchy tights under my dresses didn't keep me from feeling intense excitement each day as I walked a quarter mile down the country road to catch the school bus. I loved to read. And to write. I even liked figuring out those mind-bending math story problems. Excelling in school soon became my pastime, and I was rather competitive about it.

As my classmates and I sat working on a test, I tried my best to not only answer all of the questions correctly but also to hurry. Somehow being the first one to rise from my blond wooden desk and walk my paper up to the front of the class to flip it upside down on the teacher's desk made me feel important.

My instructor's opinion meant a great deal to me. I wanted her to think I was smart. To think I was cooperative. And kind. And so I tried my best to be all of these things. (Can you say overachiever? I knew you could.) And then I waited with anxious anticipation every time parent-teacher conferences rolled around. The only other woman I cared more about impressing besides my teacher was my sweet mother.

Now this was the seventies. Our parents would return home from the school building that night clutching a canary yellow piece of paper. On the paper was a little chart that graphed out all of the various subjects I was taking as well as the behavioral areas I was being evaluated on. Of course, reading, writing, and 'rithmetic were a big part of this evaluation, but there were also other items on the list. In addition to academics like science and social studies, there were electives such as music and art and gym.

Beyond all the course work, there were categories for classroom behavior, including things like politeness and cooperativeness with classmates. When there are thirty students in a room all trying to make a papier-mâché replica of the ancient Mayan ruins, learning to get along is crucial. Another character quality was respect. Did the student show respect not only to the teachers but also to other students? Line after line detailed the character qualities for rating the stunning student I wanted to be.

For each of the academic subjects as well as the behavioral characteristics, a teacher could check one of five boxes: *Very Good. Good. Average. Needs Improvement. Poor.* Oh, how I loved seeing all of the "Very Good" and "Good" boxes checked on the progress report my mom brought home. My identity was completely tied up in being the smart and model student. However, year after year there was one section in which I did not earn a "Very Good" or even a "Good" score. In the pesky little box called "Listening Skills," the highest rating I ever got was probably "Average" — and more often than not, I saw a big fat check mark in the "Needs Improvement" box.

"Karen is a delightful student," my teacher exclaimed as she visited with my mother during those parent-teacher powwows. "But she does seem to have a tad bit of trouble listening. Especially when I am talking." When my mother inquired whether I had trouble following instructions, the teacher assured her I had no trouble with that. (Apparently I could still take note of the instructions while my lips were moving.) The issue was my willingness to listen when the teacher was talking or another student had the floor for a minute or two. Still, I couldn't seem to keep my little jaws from flapping. I just had to add my two cents' worth. Whenever there was a gap of silence in the teacher's speech or another student's comment, you could count on me to fill in the gap. (And I'm sure, in my defense, I felt that what I had to say was way more interesting than whoever else was talking at the time, including my instructor!)

It always bummed me out when my teacher reported that I didn't listen so well and I talked too much. But it didn't bother me enough to motivate a change in my behavior. I *liked* filling those gaps. And, to tell the truth, I still do. When a group of people are chatting and there is even a small lull in the conversation, if I am not intentional about reining in my tongue, I will rush right in to fill that gap and fill it good.

Fill That Gap and Fill It Good

My husband says my ability to talk is what first attracted him to me. He loved how I could work a room, making the shy ones feel included. I could converse with the college president and yuck it up with the grocery store bag boy all in the same afternoon. Yep. My college sweetheart loved how I could talk. So this rather shy guy bought a ring, slipped it on my finger, grabbed my hand, and off we proceeded down the church aisle and into marital bliss. My proficiency at all things linguistic hadn't bothered him before. In fact, he had felt it was an asset. I talked and talked. He smiled and listened. And it really didn't seem to bother him.

Then, about three days into our honeymoon, he had this thought: "When is she *ever* gonna shut up?" In fact, if I make it to heaven before he does, he's decided just what should go on my tombstone:

A *period*.

Ask him why, and he'll declare, "Well, she'll finally be done yacking!" (He insists my language has no periods — just commas, colons, and semicolons — because there's always more to come!)

In a group Bible study or a visit with friends over coffee, I can easily monopolize the conversation. And, in the early days, I didn't even know it was happening. I just assumed everyone was as dazzled by my words as I was.

I'm not sure how I was first enlightened, but I soon came to discover that often when I was talking, other people in the room were mentally checking out. Or I noticed there were other women in the Bible study or the playgroup who never seemed to give their two cents' worth. I just couldn't figure this out. Didn't they have anything to say? Didn't they have something to add to the discussion?

Eventually, I came to realize that perhaps the problem wasn't with the other people in the group. *Gulp*. Maybe I was too ready to jump in the minute there was a gap in the conversation. Maybe the other folks needed a pause or two for their thoughts to gel before they could speak them. And maybe, just maybe, if some of us who talk too much would actually zip our lips a minute, then these people could have an opportunity to speak up more often.

I knew that things were going to have to change for me if I wanted to use my words well and shed my habit of gap filling. In fact, over the years I have developed a practice or two to help in this endeavor. The first is a little rule of thumb (or rule of tongue, perhaps). I only chime in or respond to the question thrown out by the study leader about every third time I think I have something to say. And you know what? It comes out just about right, and no one seems to suffer from not hearing the nuggets I withhold.

Here's another practice — I pause before I pipe up. It works in a group. It also works one-on-one. When the person with whom I'm chatting pauses, it doesn't always mean they have finished what they want to say. They may still be mentally composing the next sentence. When I take their pause as a green light that it's my turn to talk, I may actually be interrupting instead. No, not in a rude way — interjecting midsentence — but by butting in before they've finished their thoughts. Pausing for a moment before I pipe up helps me to be both courteous and understanding.

A person who seeks not only to listen but to understand as

well is rare — a treasure. And rare treasures are priceless. When we make listening and understanding our aim, we become valuable treasures in the lives of those around us.

Talking and Listening

The apostle James has more good advice about the tongue. "My dear brothers and sisters, take note of this: Everyone should be quick to listen, slow to speak and slow to become angry, because human anger does not produce the righteousness that God desires" (James 1:19–20).

Even if you don't consider yourself a major gap filler, perhaps you know what it's like to be someone who is "quick to speak." That's an easy trap to fall into, especially when dealing with family members. Or maybe you can relate to being "slow to listen," thinking more about what you're planning to say rather than really listening to what a friend is sharing. However, according the passage from James, listening is something we should do quickly; and when it comes to speaking, we should take our time. And I love how, for extra emphasis, James begins by saying, "My dear brothers and sisters, *take note of this . . .*" He knew we'd need to plaster this verse on a neon-colored sticky note posted right on our bathroom mirror where we are sure to see it!

When we flip-flop these two commands — being slow to listen and quick to speak — it often leads to the third part of that verse: we are quick to become angry. (Quicker sometimes than Mr. Usain Bolt. Not heard his name before? Search for him on YouTube to get the full picture. Just don't blink!)

Speaking too soon combined with not listening leads to conflict — and conflict often leads to anger. But when we choose to live out the words of this verse, the promise of Scripture is that we can defuse angry encounters before they even spark. So let's go back and see what boxes we can check on some of our elementary practices of the faith. Namely, talking and listening.

The Bible has much to say about both talking and listening. And many of these verses can be found in the Old Testament book of Proverbs. I have always loved this book, especially the pithy statements about how to live right. They're like Old Testament tweets! Here are just a few about how to use both our words and our ears:

- "When there are many words, sin is unavoidable, but the one who controls his lips is wise." (10:19 HCSB)

- "Do you see a man who speaks too soon? There is more hope for a fool than for him." (29:20 HCSB)

- "The one who gives an answer before he listens — this is foolishness and disgrace for him." (18:13 HCSB)

- "Even fools are thought wise if they keep silent, and discerning if they hold their tongues." (17:28)

When I break down these verses into foundational principles, I come up with three warnings about words and then one piece of advice. The warnings?

1. Don't speak too much.
2. Don't speak too soon.
3. Don't speak without first listening.

And then the advice? Don't speak at all.

Don't Speak Too Much

When there are many words, sin is unavoidable, but the one who controls his lips is wise. (Proverbs 10:19 HCSB)

When we rattle off words in rapid succession, we will almost certainly end up saying something that is sinful. But a person who learns to control what she says (and perhaps how many words she uses) is smart indeed.

Has your mouth ever gotten you into trouble — yes, even made you sin — all because you talked too much? In your conversation you started to ramble. The more you spoke, the more your speech dug a deep hole, tripping you up and trapping you inside. Soon you were in a mighty tangled mess. It's certainly happened to me.

I recall once visiting with a friend at a high school basketball game. Her son and my daughter, both sixteen at the time, had a bit of a crush on one another. It was nothing official, but we both thought it was sweet. As we discussed this whole new relationship and the current dating culture, I began to rattle off my opinion about things. We had tried very hard to instill in our kids not to choose someone to date, or even marry, just based on their looks. In fact, we often joke with them that looks should not matter since we are all headed toward ugly. (Of course my daughter was quick to chime in that while it is true that we are all headed toward ugly, some get there faster than others. Therefore, she wants to pick someone with a great starting point!)

In my conversation with my friend, I was just rambling on and on and really didn't give her much time to talk. In trying to express that we were happy our daughter not only chose someone who was good-looking, as this teenager was (hey, I might be getting old, but I'm not blind!), but also someone of good character who had a wonderful personality and godly habits and traits, somehow just the opposite came out. Although I didn't know it at the time, she thought I was saying we were glad our daughter was choosing on character and cared less about looks because, boy — was her son homely! This was in fact just the *opposite* of what I was actually trying to say.

It wasn't until a few days after this basketball game that I realized I had conveyed the complete opposite of what I was trying to say. I received a letter from my friend stating how hurt she was that I would give a backhanded compliment about her son's character while at the same time basically saying he was unattractive. I was floored. And devastated. And misunderstood. And now I had a fractured friendship with someone I'd really hoped I could hang out with. All because my words were too many.

I called her up immediately to apologize and to state what I'd meant to say before my rambling and roaming thoughts came out as misspoken words that led to misunderstanding, conflict, and offense.

If we want to avoid offending our friends — or committing any number of verbal sins — we need to learn to control our lips. And taking a first step can be simpler than you might imagine. When we sense the Holy Spirit telling us that things are starting to go downhill, we can simply say, "I'm sorry. I'm talking too much." And then? We can "shut our tater trap," as my dad used to say when I was little. (And yes, for those of you old enough to recognize it, he learned that phrase from Festus on *Gunsmoke*!) However, before we can listen to the nudge of the Holy Spirit tapping on our hearts and telling us to zip our lips, we must have an attitude of prayer throughout the day that enables him to do just that. As a Facebook image I saw recently declared, we must ask God to "Put your arm around my shoulders and your hand over my mouth!"

Don't Speak Too Soon

Do you see a man who speaks too soon?
There is more hope for a fool than for him.
(Proverbs 29:20 HCSB)

Speaking too soon. Before all the facts are out. Before we really understand those facts. Before we've listened fully to the other side. And most importantly, before we've had time to pray and process what we've heard with the Lord. When we do any one or even a combination of those things, we are foolish.

Scripture has many things to say about fools. They are senseless, lacking in understanding, rebellious, and can suffer affliction because of their choices. They hate knowledge. They are wayward. Simpletons. Complacent and shameful. They do not listen to instruction, and as a result they come to ruin. Their way seems right to them, but it leads to disaster. They show their annoyance at once and refuse to overlook an insult. Don't know about you, but that's not a list of descriptions I want tacked on to my public profile!

In order not to speak too soon, we need to cultivate two habits: perfecting the art of the pause and pondering.

Perfect the art of the pause. Pausing creates white space in a conversation that enables us to sort out our thoughts before we let out our words. Perhaps you've heard the old "count to ten" advice. Although it may sound silly, I know from experience it can help. Counting to ten before responding provides just enough wiggle room to really think through what we are about to say, sometimes realizing in that short pause the ridiculousness of the words we were about to let out of the trapdoor of our soul.

Ponder what the other person said and perhaps go on a fact-finding mission. How easy it is to jump to conclusions when we don't have all of the facts. Holding our tongues, and our opinions, for a while often gives us time to assess the situation clearly before pronouncing judgment. In fact, if you are in the middle of a heated discussion with someone and they ask, "Well, what do you think?" it is perfectly reasonable to tell them you don't yet know what you think. Yes, this may frustrate some people. They may think you're copping out. They may even accuse you of not knowing your own mind. But I have found that many times what I was going to say (but thankfully didn't!) was not in the end what I wanted to express. Giving our thoughts time to settle and soak in Scripture is a wonderful habit that will keep us from answering too soon and looking foolish.

So pause. Gather facts. Think before you answer. Do not speak too soon.

Don't Speak without First Listening

The one who gives an answer before he listens —
> this is foolishness and disgrace for him. (Proverbs
> 18:13 HCSB)

My youngest son loves to tell a good story. He reenacts every detail with his body and facial expressions as well as the inflections in his voice. He typically tells me these stories just after he's come through the back kitchen door and tossed his backpack on our wooden bench. I'm usually doing dishes, mixing up the meat loaf, or sorting through the day's mail.

As he launches into his reenactment full force, I nod and give the occasional "Uh-huh," and "Oh, really?" but my man-cub is wise to my distraction — he can tell whether or not I am really listening. Sometimes he calls me out by asking me to repeat back to him what he just said. (Drat! Why did I do the same thing to my kids when they were younger? Now they know my trick.) He picks up on my cues that tell whether I am really engaged with my ears and my eyes and my brain or whether I am simply faking it.

The authors of Proverbs urge us to really listen to the other person before responding, thereby saving ourselves from looking foolish (again!). Do you see how closely our words are linked to our looking like a fool or bringing disgrace?

Listening is more than just being quiet for a moment. It's not just the pause we were talking about earlier. Listening includes paying attention to the whole person, and especially their emotions. When we really listen, we give careful attention not just to the words a person says but also to the feelings he or she is trying to communicate. Listening requires attending to the other person's heart. So how do we do that?

The skill of repeating or mirroring what someone has just said can be quite helpful here. Every once in a while, stop and repeat back to the person what you think you are hearing them say. For example, "So I think what I am hearing you say is that although you are invited to the party, you're not sure if Annie really wants you to come, and this is making you hesitant to go. Is that what you mean?" The value of mirroring is that it not only demonstrates to the other person that you're listening, it also helps to clarify that you are accurately understanding what's been said.

In fact, clarifying questions are essential to good listening. Michael, our life group leader, does this regularly in our group conversations. For example, he might ask someone to elaborate on a word or phrase. If they said they felt sad about something, he might ask them to elaborate on what they mean by the word *sad*. What kind of sad? Why do they think it made them feel sad? What could've happened differently that would have made them feel happy instead?

In addition to asking clarifying questions, Michael has also taught our group how to listen for what he calls "heart drops." This is when a person drops a hint about something deeper going on in her heart without really coming out and saying it directly. Maybe from her conversation you sense that she's feeling rejection. Or loneliness. Or that she feels inadequate.

If you sense a heart drop, acknowledge it by asking for more information: "Go back to when you were talking about your father never going to your games when you were young. How did that make you feel? How do you think it might be affecting you today?" Then shut your mouth, and let her do the talking. Picking up on someone's heart drop is a great way to help her express herself more directly. One caution: resist the temptation to put words in someone's mouth. If you sense a heart drop, don't say to the person, "So ... What I hear you saying is that you feel lonely and rejected and like you are a loser in life? Is that right?" Trust me. That will not help that person or your relationship with her at all! Instead, focus on the emotion by asking open-ended questions — questions to which you do not know the answer.

Yes, learn to really listen before you speak. It will not only save you heartache, but it will help others to express their hearts as well.

Don't Speak at All

> Even fools are thought wise if they keep silent,
> and discerning if they hold their tongues. (Proverbs 17:28)

Boy oh boy, is this hard for all of us who are gap fillers! Sometimes we just can't stand a moment of silence in a conversation. We fidget. And fuss. And soon we blurt out *something* just because we can't stand the awkwardness of silence. However, silence is more than golden. It can also be God-sent. He might use it to give us some breathing space, a brief interlude that allows us to process the conversation or pay attention to the emotions behind the words. I find it interesting that not all cultures view silence as awkward. Some pass long stretches of time just being together. No words. No worry. Just complete quiet. To them what feels strange is when someone tries to fill up all the silence with speech!

Publilius Syrus, a Roman writer in the first century BC, is quoted as saying, "I have often regretted my speech, never my silence." I love the way the Amplified Version of the Bible expresses this truth: "Even a fool when he holds his peace is considered wise; when he closes his lips he is esteemed a man of understanding" (Proverbs 17:28).

Yes, sometimes the best thing to say is nothing at all.

We have been close friends with a couple for nearly thirty years. The husband, Richard, is a very quiet man. I can't ever remember him saying something offensive. In fact, I don't remember him saying much at all because he is usually pretty quiet. (Unless of course you bring up a subject near and dear to both of our hearts, which is the Detroit Tigers. Then we could chat for hours.) I've always thought how great it is that Richard doesn't have a lot of words to regret. At least not ones I know about. But there is another asset to Richard being the strong, silent type; when he does speak, people almost always listen. When he had something to say in a Bible study we both once attended, it was usually a great point. And honestly? Even though others in the group (ahem … me!) talked more frequently and used more flowery and theological terms, often it was Richard's words that stood out. Because he doesn't just drone on and on all of the time sounding like the teacher in a Charlie Brown cartoon, when he does have something to say, people tend to listen.

Some of us just need to accept the fact that it is often perfectly fine to say nothing at all. Yes, we don't have to use fancy words and big terms or convincing arguments to be thought of as smart. We just need to learn to keep it shut. *Who knew?*

These "Old Testament tweets" offer punchy, practical bits of advice that — if followed — allow us not only to temper our tongues, but also to strengthen relationships. Do you feel one of them might help in your life right now? Have you been talking too much or speaking too soon? Did you answer before really listening or fail to remain silent when now you wish you had zipped it? What impact did it have on a friendship or your relationship with a family member or coworker?

I've struggled with all of these situations at various times — most recently with the whole "speaking too soon" routine.

My sixteen-year-old son had a baseball game last week. Upon returning home that night he walked by me in the kitchen, and I noticed that the back pocket on his uniform had something round in it — round like a tin of chewing tobacco! I opened my mouth and promptly let loose, accusing and lecturing in classic mama form: "What in the world? Chewing tobacco? Not only is that stuff cancer causing, it is illegal for people your age! You are in big trouble, buddy. Give that to me now!"

He looked at me a bit cockeyed as he slowly smiled and reached into his back pocket — which I found odd for a sixteen-year-old boy about to have one bummer of a summer due to being placed on house arrest.

He concealed his hand behind his back for a few seconds and then when he finally forked it over, I saw the reason for his grin. It was a tin all right — a tin of "cool watermelon mints"!

My little jump-to-conclusion lecture taught me something: I need to get better at asking questions before I hurl accusations. Or better yet, ask questions, listen patiently to the answers, and then don't accuse at all!

Investigate? Uh-huh.

Process and pray? Oh yes.

Pronounce a loss of privilege to a child? Perhaps.

But *not* speak words I'll regret before I have all the facts.

Less talk, more listening. Yep. That's what we need. We may also need a little listening lesson in another crucial area — our relationship with God.

Listening to God

Not only is it a bad habit to talk too much (and to talk before we really listen), but I have also discovered something else about my "Just-gotta-have-the-next-(and of course the last)-word" behavior. It often means this: not only am I not listening to the person I am with. I am also not listening to God.

When I yack too much, I can't hear him whisper to me what I should — and should not — be saying. I can't ask God about the answer he might want me to give to questions I'm being asked. Instead, I'm focused only on expressing my opinions and exerting my will. Which reminds me of another truth about talking too much: "A [self-confident] fool has no delight in understanding but only in revealing his personal opinions *and* himself" (Proverbs 18:2 AMP).

Ouch!

How about you? How do you rate in the listening, talking, and expressing-your-own-opinion departments? Think back on your last few conversations. Did you seek to really understand the other person? Or were you more concerned with getting your words out first? Did you make an intentional effort to listen to God as you were conversing with others, taking your cues from him about what you should and shouldn't say? Or were you focused on asserting your own opinions?

Question: If those closest to you were asked, which would they say more accurately describes you: a great listener or a constant chatterbox? Has not really listening to the other person (or failing to listen to God as you were talking with someone) ever caused you trouble? What happened? If you could have do-overs, how would you go back and handle the interaction differently?

Wanna take a double-dog dare? For the next twenty-four to

forty-eight hours, make an effort to really listen to the people in your life. Purpose to not give your opinion unless you are directly asked. Instead, seek to ask clarifying questions that will help you better understand what the other person is expressing. Beyond that, keep your thoughts to yourself. See if anyone comments on the difference they see in you. (My family always asks if I have laryngitis!)

Let's pinky promise today that we will seek to be quick to listen and slow to speak — not the other way around. Our family and friends will thank us for it. And they might just get a word in edgewise!

I know you can do it. With a little effort, energized with the power of the Holy Spirit, we can all better learn to Keep. It. Shut.

4

ZIP IT
AND PRAY

How to Talk to God
Before You Talk to Others

Prayer will make a man cease from sin,
or sin will entice a man to cease from prayer.

JOHN BUNYAN

When I was in college in the 1980s, I came across a pamphlet entitled "How to Spend an Hour in Prayer." I had been a Christian for just a couple of years, and I was intrigued. I knew about people called prayer warriors who placed great emphasis on conversing with God, and prayer seemed to come to them as naturally as breathing. Maybe you know some prayer warriors too. They constantly want to know your prayer requests. They habitually intercede for others. For them, spending an hour in prayer is no big thing.

I myself have never been known as a prayer warrior. Ever. In fact, I am more like a prayer wimp. I find it difficult to keep my thoughts from wandering when I pray. They ricochet all over the place as I try to focus on communicating with God.

Way back in the eighties when I came across that pamphlet, I decided that things were going to change. So I took off to a park one sunny, autumn afternoon with my Bible in hand and a resolve in my heart to follow the step-by-step guide. I felt like a spiritual giant.

I settled myself on a quaint park bench near some pine trees and a lovely flower garden. I opened my Bible and looked down at my pamphlet and began to do what it suggested: "Spend five minutes thanking God for the blessings in your life. Spend five minutes praising God for his character qualities," and so on. Apparently, breaking down the various categories into five-minute increments was supposed to help. But it didn't help me. Five minutes seemed like an eternity.

Pretty soon a jogger happened by. He was carrying a small portable radio — without headphones — and the blaring music distracted me. I couldn't really get into worshiping the Lord with Michael Jackson's "Beat It" blaring in my ears. (Hmm ... maybe in retrospect I should have joined along, singing that tune out loud to the devil!)

Two hyper squirrels decided to chase each other up and down a tree and around and around my bench. I laughed at their antics but again lost my place. A family having a picnic nearby decided to engage in a rousing game of Frisbee. The Frisbee got away from one of the children and soared past me, barely missing my head. Even when the animals and humans quieted down, still I had trouble concentrating. I couldn't focus. I kept thinking of all the things I had to do back at the dorm. And I got distracted looking around at nature, even though it wasn't making a sound. I gave up after twenty-three minutes and concluded I just wasn't cut out to be a prayer warrior.

My prayer wimp status makes me feel spiritually inferior to those for whom prayer comes naturally, but it doesn't stop there — a lack of prayer affects another area of my life. When I don't pray, I am more likely to say things I later regret. Or to say something that needs to be said but I say it in the wrong way or at the wrong time. And there are even times that I say nothing at all when I should really be speaking up. Yes, when I don't make it a habit to talk to God, I sometimes speak (or fail to speak) to others in a way I later regret.

Talking to God helps me know how to talk to others.

More Prayer = Less Gossip

In addition to the fact that prayer warriors take communicating with God seriously, I have also noticed something else about them. They are not generally known for gossiping, using harsh words, or talking too much. In fact, just the opposite is true. Could there be a correlation between the time and effort spent talking with God and the quality of our conversations with others? I think so.

Take my friend Kelly. She and I became close friends over thirty years ago when we were fresh out of high school and both landed on the same floor in our tiny midwestern Christian college dorm. She was on the cheerleading squad. I was on the dance team. She had only sisters. I had only a brother. Her favorite color is lavender. Mine is peach. But the greatest difference between Kelly and me? My mouth has often gotten me into trouble. However, in the thirty years I have known Kelly, I am certain I have never once heard her gossip. Seriously! While she seemed to spend a lot of time talking to the Lord, she did not spend time talking about others. Or talking in an angry way. Or saying the wrong thing. Or talking too much. I don't ever recall her having to remove her foot from her mouth, something I seemed to have to do often during my college days.

As I got to know her, I noticed right away that she took her relationship with Christ very seriously. Oh, she wasn't one to do acts of righteousness before others so that she could be thought of as super spiritual. I just noticed things. Like the fact that she often had her Bible open on her dorm bed, where she had high-lighted passages (with a lavender highlighter, of course!). Or I would spot her writing in her prayer journal, recording requests from family and friends that she had promised to pray for. She often sent me a note in the campus mail, telling me she was praying specifically for me. The more I got to know her, the more I realized just how important prayer was to my friend Kelly.

Watching Kelly's life over the years has convinced me that there is a direct correlation between our prayer life and our con-versations. Perhaps if we spent more time and energy on our prayer life, we would use our tongues more wisely.

Processing Life through Prayer

My husband, Todd, has also taught me about the impact of taking prayer seriously. He often gets up early in the morning to pray. And, when he was a small group leader, he frequently stopped by the church after his late-night shift at the factory just to walk around the circle of chairs in our classroom, praying for each person in our small group. If I had just worked a ten-hour shift at a factory getting off at 2:00 a.m., the last thing I would do is go on a little, private prayer walk. I would drive straight home and dive into my comfy bed, vowing to pray in the morning. But not Todd. Over the years, he has consistently forged his rela-tionship with God through regular prayer times — that's how he processes life. And if it means losing out on a little sleep, so be it.

Interestingly enough, Todd, like Kelly, does not have a prob-lem with his tongue. Very rarely have I ever heard him talk negatively about someone else. Very rarely has he said something for which he needed to go back and apologize. Very rarely does he talk too much in group settings, monopolizing the conversation and turning off those who are listening. His life is evidence of a tight connection between processing life in conversation with God and using wisdom and restraint in conversations with everyone else.

I wish I were more naturally like Todd and other prayer warriors who instinctively turn first to prayer to process life. But my default mode typically looks something more like this:

A concern arises.

I mull it over in my mind.

I pick up the phone or write an email to process the concern with a close friend.

I take the friend's counsel and advice into consideration.

I mull over the concern some more. And some more. And then some more.

I feel completely muddled.

Suddenly, it occurs to me that perhaps I should actually pray about it. So, almost as a last resort, I finally consult God.

Why, oh, why is my default mode not to run to God first? To hit my knees *before* I hit the phone — or tap away on the keyboard? Though my natural inclination is to process *before* I pray, I am continually reminding myself to flip that script — with a sticky note posted near my kitchen sink and a screen saver on my phone, both sporting the same phrase — "But wait. Have you prayed about it?" We are better poised to process life's troubles after petitioning God first. I'm still learning this lesson, but the calm I feel when I get the order straight encourages me to keep on trying.

Perhaps you have people in your life who are like Kelly and Todd — those whose lives demonstrate a connection between prayer and using words wisely. But what does the Bible have to say about this connection? Let's take a trip back in time and spy on someone who made prayer a regular habit and as a result seemed to know just what to say — and do.

Role Models in Babylon

A long time ago (606 BC, to be exact), King Nebuchadnezzar of Babylon captured the city of Jerusalem. The Babylonians stole some of the sacred objects from the temple of God to take back with them to their homeland. But it wasn't just sacred relics they carried back with them. They captured a few Judean teenagers and whisked them away to Babylon too. Among this group of youths, four young men stood out for their intellect and athleticism, and they were selected to enter a training program to work for the Babylonian empire. Now you might think that being selected as the cream of the crop would be a good thing. However, the honor also came with some challenges for these young Israelites.

To start off, they were given different names. Instead of Daniel, Hananiah, Mishael, and Azariah, they were called Belteshazzar, Shadrach, Meshach, and Abednego. They also had to learn to speak a new language and become familiar with the culture and literature of the land. And as they entered a three-year training process, they were told they'd have to make changes to their diets.

Daniel and his friends were given daily portions of the choicest food and fine wine from the king's own royal kitchens. Although the biblical text doesn't provide specifics, the young men determined that the food was ceremonially unclean and that eating it would have violated God's law. Instead of arguing with the king, however, the young men proposed an alternative:

"Please test your servants for ten days: Give us nothing but vegetables to eat and water to drink. Then compare our appearance with that of the young men who eat the royal food, and treat your servants in accordance with what you see." So he agreed to this and tested them for ten days. At the end of the ten days they looked healthier and better nourished than any of the young men who ate the royal food. So the guard took away their choice food and the wine they were to drink and gave them vegetables instead. (Daniel 1:12–16)

Their countercultural menu of just veggies and H_2O worked. By refusing the king's choice morsels, they honored the one true King. And, although Daniel limited his intake of rich foods, he indulged himself richly in something else. Prayer.

As the story of Daniel unfolds, we see that the four young men continue to make very wise choices. They gain a reputation for impeccable character and great knowledge (Daniel 1:20). Because Daniel was able to interpret dreams for the king, he became a trusted adviser (Daniel 2). It seems no one around could find any fault with these young men. But then comes trouble.

King Nebuchadnezzar got a notion to build a statue — an idol, no less — on the plain of Dura in the province of Babylon. And it wasn't just some standard-issue, cheap metal structure. No, this statue would be covered with gold and stand ninety feet tall and nine feet wide (roughly equivalent to the height of a nine-story building). Kind of hard to miss. And this monumental statue wouldn't be just a passing tourist attraction. A herald loudly decreed that people of all races, nations, and languages, whenever they heard the sound of the royal musical instruments, were to bow down to worship the massive statue. And those who didn't would suffer a swift death by fiery furnace.

This posed a little problem for Shadrach, Meshach, and Abednego, who bowed down only to the one true God. And so whenever they heard the music, they refused to drop to their knees. On hearing of their refusal, the king flew into a rage. He ordered that the three friends not only be thrown into the furnace, but that it be heated to seven times hotter than usual. *Uh-oh!*

So the young men were bound and thrown into the fire. But they did not burn up! In fact, when witnesses peered into the fire, they saw not only the three men walking around unbound and unharmed, they also saw a fourth person who appeared divine. When the three friends emerged, not a hair on their heads was singed, nor did their clothing smell of smoke. God had miraculously protected and rescued them.

Later, Daniel also faced a life-threatening situation. Jealous of his success, some administrators and princes searched for faults in Daniel, but they couldn't find one single thing to criticize. He was always faithful, honest, and responsible, making them look bad by comparison. They decided that their only chance of finding fault would be in connection with Daniel's faith in God.

So they concocted a little plan. They convinced the current king (now Darius) to issue an order that for thirty days anyone who prayed to any person or god but the king would be thrown into the den of lions. Of course, they knew this would trap Daniel, because he was well-known for his habit of praying to the God of Israel. We pop in on the story in Daniel 6:10–12:

> Now when Daniel learned that the decree had been published, he went home to his upstairs room where the windows opened toward Jerusalem. Three times a day he got down on his knees and prayed, giving thanks to

his God, just as he had done before. Then these men went as a group and found Daniel praying and asking God for help. So they went to the king and spoke to him about his royal decree: "Did you not publish a decree that during the next thirty days anyone who prays to any god or human being except to you, Your Majesty, would be thrown into the lions' den?"

King Darius replied affirmatively. But then he was given the awful news that it was Daniel who had violated the decree. This meant he had to be thrown to the hungry lions. Now Darius was quite fond of Daniel, and he looked for a way to get him out of this predicament, but to no avail. The decree had been signed. It was a done deal. And so Daniel was thrown to the ferocious felines. Nevertheless, the king did not abandon hope. He refused his usual nightly entertainment and spent a sleepless night fasting.

Although he likely expected the worst, in the morning the king beheld a wonderful sight. Daniel had not been devoured! He was alive and well. The king then tossed into the lions' den not just the men who had maliciously accused Daniel but also their wives and children. Scripture reveals that the lions devoured the bodies before they even hit the floor. Then King Darius posted this status on his royal Facebook page (Well, sort of!):

"I issue a decree that in every part of my kingdom people must fear and reverence the God of Daniel.

"For he is the living God
   and he endures forever;
his kingdom will not be destroyed,
   his dominion will never end.

> He rescues and he saves;
>> he performs signs and wonders
>> in the heavens and on the earth.
>
> He has rescued Daniel
>> from the power of the lions."
>> (Daniel 6:26–27)

Daniel's commitment to prayer saved him from destruction and made God famous.

Learning from Daniel

Now, what in the world does the story of Daniel and his friends have to do with us? Some of us may relocate to a strange new country with unfamiliar customs and foods, but I doubt any of us will be tossed into a roaring fire or face a roaring lion. Does Daniel's saga hold any life lessons for us? At least three that I spy.

1. Surround Yourself with Like-Minded Friends

Although Joseph remained faithful to God in a foreign culture, most of us — Daniel included — need a little help from our friends. Standing in solidarity, Daniel, Shadrach, Meshach, and Abednego agreed together to stay faithful to God's law by forgoing the unclean foods. We teach our children to choose their friends wisely and not give into peer pressure to do something wrong, but then so often we forget to heed our own advice. The apostle Paul warns us of this, "Do not be misled: 'Bad company corrupts good character'" (1 Corinthians 15:33). However, the converse is also true. Being around those who share our faith and conviction can strengthen and encourage us to choose wisely and avoid sin. The author of Hebrews writes: "See to it, brothers and sisters, that none of you has a sinful, unbelieving heart that turns away from the living God. But encourage one another daily, as long as it is called 'Today,' so that none of you may be hardened by sin's deceitfulness" (Hebrews 3:12–13). My son's Russian friend David, told me a saying about this from his culture: "Show me who your friends are, and I will show you who you are."

If we fail to be intentional in choosing friends who make godly choices, and instead surround ourselves with those who make poor or even ungodly ones, those friends and their poor choices can rub off on us. If we aren't firm in our convictions, we might buckle, becoming like them. This includes how a person uses their words.

I once knew a woman who regularly spoke ill of her spouse. She never seemed to have anything positive to say about his behavior or his personality. My husband and I both knew this guy well and we thought he was wonderful. He was soft-spoken and kind. Generous and loyal.

The negative-word-wielding woman and I had a mutual friend. This friend told me she'd stopped spending time with Ms. Hubby-Basher because whenever she did, she found she was more likely to complain about her own husband too. The constant criticizing she experienced seemed to give her permission to rattle off her own list of complaints about her man. She finally distanced herself from this combative lady and started spending time with other wives — ones who were not card-carrying members of the Husband Haters Club.

2. Watch Your Intake

Even though Daniel and his friends found themselves in a culture that not only saw nothing wrong with eating food from the king's table but considered it an honor, they did not give in to the Babylonians' pagan practices. Because they were obedient and didn't defile themselves with unclean food, the fruit of their lives was evident. God blessed them with wisdom and understanding far exceeding that of anyone else.

It's a principle I learned in the early days of computers when I was just in high school: "Garbage in, garbage out." GIGO for short. In other words, poor inputs lead to poor outputs. The same principle applies to our struggle with words. If we feed our minds a steady diet of cultural "garbage" — entertainment or social media that compromises biblical values — we can be sure those inputs will leak out in what we say.

That is not to say we should avoid all media, but we must be aware how what we "input" influences what we "output." For example, while I am pretty particular (and somewhat restrictive) when it comes to the movies I watch, very rarely I'll view one that includes some foul language. I absolutely hate that a movie with a wonderful lesson might also include some profanity. But do you know what I hate more? The fact that although I am not a cussing Christian, sometimes these bad words continue to pop into my brain for a few days after I see that film. For some people like me, hearing vulgar speech or negative conversations predisposes us to speak that way ourselves. (I know this isn't the case for everyone. My husband hears a steady stream of foul language at the factory where he works. This doesn't seem to affect him the same way it would me. Perhaps God dishes out an extra measure of grace to people who must endure such situations.)

Maybe we should take a clue from Daniel and commit to obedience to God first, watching our intake and refusing those things that represent garbage in our lives.

Sometimes bad speech slithers stealthily into our vocabulary, even if the speech is only in our heads. Without realizing it, we pick up the language we are exposed to. I live in the Midwest, but when I visit North Carolina a few times a year, I pick up a cultural catchphrase.

I start to say "Y'all."

Here in Michigan, we don't usually say "Y'all" when talking to someone. Or say "All y'all" when talking to a group — which I'm told is the plural of "y'all"! We Michiganders say, "You guys," (which incessantly annoys my sweet-tea-sippin' Southern friends. They'll say, "You guys? *What?* We're all women here. There isn't a guy in the bunch!") Yes, when I head south and hang around these ladies, I begin to pick up their lingo.

Are you listening to a symphony of sarcasm as you watch a sitcom? Are you experiencing steamy scenarios on the pages of that novel now sitting on your nightstand? You might want to rethink exposing yourself to such pastimes or they could become part of your thought patterns and maybe even your actions and speech.

3. Make Prayer a Daily Priority

Did you notice that when Daniel's enemies tried to trap him he was already known as a man who made prayer a daily priority? "Three times a day he got down on his knees and prayed, giving thanks to his God, just as he had done before" (Daniel 6:10). He didn't suddenly start praying to God because he was in a sticky situation; he *continued* his habit of praying to God. He spoke to God constantly, and as a result he didn't fumble and stumble over his words when asked to do something that violated his faith. He simply spoke the truth and allowed God to deal with the consequences. And Daniel's buddies did the same. When commanded to bow their knee to the gold statue, they refused. Their allegiance, both in word and in actions, was first to God.

When the person we talk to most is our heavenly Father, we naturally become more concerned with what he thinks of our words and actions than with what others think of them. When conversation with God is at the top of our priority list, we will have a better chance of speaking the truth when asked to do something that compromises biblical values.

Chances are, our fiery furnace or lions' den equivalent isn't a physical one but a social one. We may be tempted to join in on an ungodly conversation with a group of friends. If we opt out — if we do not participate in the climate of criticism and negativity — we may be tossed aside and feel the fire of rejection from others. However, I have found that when my relationship with God is solid and I make prayer a daily priority, I care much more about pleasing him than pleasing others.

Are you someone who never struggles to make prayer time a priority? Me neither. But I have acquired a few trusted tips and spiritual strategies that, when implemented, can enable us to be a little more warrior and a lot less wimp.

More Prayer Warrior, Less Prayer Wimp

For those of us to whom prayer does not come naturally, how can we learn to process life through prayer rather than just going it on our own? Is there a direct correlation between how (and how often) we talk to God and how we talk to others?

I say a resounding yes!

I know from experience that when I carve out a chunk of time each day to consistently connect with God in prayer, I am less likely to lose patience with my kids or snap at the mister. PLEASE NOTE: I am not always consistent with prayer. I have dry times. And I have too-much-to-do-today times. I forget or get distracted. I decide to get ahead in my work rather than pray. Or I decide I'd rather flop on the couch to watch a hilarious rerun of *Family Matters* that I've laughed through twelve times already!

"Did I do that?"

Sorry — I just love Steve Urkel.

Wait. Where was I? (See I told you I get easily distracted!)

Oh yeah ... prayer.

Prayer isn't some magic pill we just pop with a quick drop to our knees, and there is no guarantee we will behave well verbally after we've uttered our "Amen." However, I do experience a calmed heart after having spent time with God — one that helps me speak in a hushed tone when I'm tempted to be harsh. Or at times my prayer time might include praying a few Scripture verses out loud. Later that day, the exact verse I prayed is the one my mind needs to recall to give me guidance in what I should and shouldn't say in a particular situation.

Here are a few steps I have learned over the years to be a little more prayer warrior and a little less prayer wimp.

1. Pray Your To-Do List

Sometimes the pressing demands of the day make it hard to hear the Lord's voice. We stress and obsess about our to-do list and all of our many appointments and responsibilities. When I have one of those days, instead of trying to banish all thoughts of what I have to do, I actually take my to-do list into my prayer time!

To pray your to-do list, find a few moments to be alone and quiet. Ask God to bring to mind all that you must accomplish that day. Make a list of everything that comes to mind. Then briefly pray through each item on the list. If more tasks come to mind, simply add them to the list. Don't worry that it is unspiritual to stop halfway through a prayer and jot down an item. If you're like me, it will help you to clear your mind and enable you to focus better on your time alone with God. He is concerned about all the details of your life, even the errands.

2. Be Intentional

Treat your time alone with God as serious as any other appointment you have. When you have to go to the dentist, you brush your teeth and make sure you show up on time for your appointment. Why do we assume our time alone with God will just happen spontaneously or in the cracks? Treat it with intentionality. Write down in your planner the time you will spend with God or set an alert on your phone. Have a plan for what you will read in the Bible or whether you will write in a journal or listen to worship music.

3. Read and Write

Get a quality devotional book or Bible study workbook that provides a Bible reading plan. But don't stop at just reading the Bible. Write down your thoughts in response to what you read. Keeping a journal — whether it is a paper one or a digital file on your computer — will help you invest in your relationship with God. You can process your life with him as you write out your thoughts. And you can both read and write prayers. The book of Psalms is sometimes referred to as the prayer book of the Bible. Read the psalms out loud to God, allowing the words to become your own. Then write out your own specific prayers to him as well. It will amaze you when you go back later and see the ways that God answered your prayers.

4. Make a Recording and Memorize

Use a smartphone app or online program such as Audacity to record yourself reading out loud any verses or passages of Scripture you would like to memorize. Then load them on an iPod, phone, or MP3 player. Pop in the earbuds and listen to the verses each day as you walk, do housework, or cook dinner. Memorizing is so much easier this way!

TOP TEN VERSES TO HELP YOU WATCH YOUR WORDS

Here are ten fabulous verses to keep in mind—or to cement in mind by memorizing them—that can help you watch your words so they don't do damage to others, to yourself, or to God.

- Words from the mouth of the wise are gracious,
  but fools are consumed by their own lips. (Ecclesiastes 10:12)

- Whoever would love life and see good days must keep their tongue from evil and their lips from deceitful speech. (1 Peter 3:10)

- Those who consider themselves religious and yet do not keep a tight rein on their tongues deceive themselves, and their religion is worthless. (James 1:26)

- May these words of my mouth and this meditation of my heart
  be pleasing in your sight,
  Lord, my Rock and my Redeemer. (Psalm 19:14)

- Let your conversation be always full of grace, seasoned with salt, so that you may know how to answer everyone. (Colossians 4:6)

- Do not let your mouth lead you into sin. (Ecclesiastes 5:6)

- Set a guard over my mouth, Lord;
  keep watch over the door of my lips. (Psalm 141:3)

- Do not let any unwholesome talk come out of your mouths, but only what is helpful for building others up according to their needs, that it may benefit those who listen. (Ephesians 4:29)

- Before a word is on my tongue,
  you, Lord, know it completely. (Psalm 139:4)

- Though you probe my heart,
  though you examine me at night and test me,
  you will find that I have planned no evil;
  my mouth has not transgressed. (Psalm 17:3)

5. Identify and Apply the Bible's Nonnegotiables

Here is an approach I have loved using over the years because it makes Scripture leap off the page and Velcro itself to my mind.

Sit down with a Bible and a notebook. Pick a New Testament book such as James or Colossians. Read it through unhurriedly, stopping each time you see a nonnegotiable command. For example:

> My dear brothers and sisters, take note of this: Everyone should be quick to listen, slow to speak and slow to become angry, because human anger does not produce the righteousness that God desires. Therefore, get rid of all moral filth and the evil that is so prevalent and humbly accept the word planted in you, which can save you. (James 1:19–21)

Did you notice there are lots of commands in this passage? Here is what you might write down in your notebook:

When dealing with others, I need to be:

- Willing to listen right off the bat
- Not in a hurry to speak (or especially to voice my opinion!)
- Patient, trying not to boil over with anger — flying off the handle doesn't accomplish anything that God desires

I must also:

- Do away with anything immoral or wicked
- Spend time imbedding Scripture in my heart in a humble way. It will save me!

After writing out the commands in your own words, jot down a few sentences of reflection based on what the verse says. Are there any action steps you might take in order to act on what the verse or verses command? Any behavioral changes or attitude adjustments required?

When we read the Bible, we learn. However, when we write out biblical commands in a way that is personal to us, we allow the Word to take root deep within our hearts. This will help us the next time we are faced with a challenging situation and need to use words wisely. When we have trained our brain to recall and apply biblical nonnegotiables, we are equipped to speak, act, and react in ways that honor God.

Will you make prayer your practice and obeying biblical commands your goal? When you do, you will be less likely to regret what you say. God's Word is both powerful and practical. Through it he will give you directives, but not without also giving you the supernatural strength to carry them out.

Perhaps we will never be faced with a roaring lion or feel the licking flames of a fiery furnace. But we will most certainly face adversity of some kind or be tempted at times to wield our tongues for evil.

Like Daniel, by forging our faith daily through the practice of prayer, we will be more readily equipped to speak and act in ways that not only save us from disaster, but also make God famous.

A little more warrior. A lot less wimp. That's my particular prayer for both of us today.

5 MOTIVES AND MANNERS

It's Not Just What You Say;
It's Why and How You Say It

> " 'Ooh, dear, how are you? Frosting in a can—so much easier
> than homemade. Look in that refrigerator. Whoa, smells like
> there wasn't anything good in here for a while.' "
>
> DEBRA, IMITATING HER MOTHER-IN-LAW, MARIE,
> ON *EVERYBODY LOVES RAYMOND*

Perhaps my all-time favorite television show is the classic sitcom *Everybody Loves Raymond.* My youngest son and I still enjoy watching reruns of this series together. The antics of the Long Island Barone family make for hilarious viewing, and the relationship between Debra and her mother-in-law, Marie, always makes me laugh out loud. Debra and Marie have all the stereotypical daughter-in-law vs. mother-in-law conflicts. Debra gets slighted and left out. Marie is dominant and gets her way. Whether it is Debra's inept parenting, bland cooking, or inadequate housecleaning, Marie never fails to offer her opinion. Whenever she's confronted about her backhanded comments, Marie always asserts that everything she says and does is motivated by love. She only corrects Debra's parenting because she cares about her grandchildren and wants them raised properly. She only makes snide remarks about Debra's culinary skills (or lack thereof) because she wants her son's family to eat good food. And of course all of her remarks about Debra's poor housekeeping skills are only her generous attempts to be helpful. Her words may come across as harsh, but she insists that everything is said in love. *Really?* Is she lying, or does she somehow actually believe her words are loving?

The sad truth is, Marie is self-deceived. And she isn't the only one who's blind to the impact and motives of her own behavior. Sometimes we have the same issue. We might be convinced our words and actions come from the very purest of motives, but do they really? Even when we speak the truth or accurately assess a situation with a family member or friend, our motives can still be dead wrong. The truth may be that my friend has an improvement to make, but is my motive for mentioning it to help her change, or to point out that I, by comparison, don't have that same fault?

When it comes to our words, what matters is not just that they are true. Of course, we should always seek to speak the truth. However, we must also examine the *why* behind the words as well as *how* we say them. When it comes to our speech, both motives and manners matter.

Multilevel Motives

My husband and I sat with our two guests in the tiny living room of our very first home. I was holding our infant son. He was our second-born child with a three-year-old sister, and I was a proud stay-at-home mother (emphasis on the proud). My husband worked for a local reconditioned appliance and furniture store, and we lived on a budget so tight it nearly squeaked. In order to make ends meet, I nursed my babies instead of buying formula, made my own baby food in a blender, and used cloth diapers rather than disposable. Of course, all of these things were good for both the baby and the environment, but mainly they were good for our wallet. I became an expert at cutting both coupons and corners. I cooked from scratch and even made my own baby wipes. I was determined to make any sacrifice that would enable me to stay at home with our children full-time.

As I sat on the couch next to my husband, I listened to the energetic young couple who was visiting with us that night. We were new to their church and they were new to our circle of friends. Both worked full-time outside the home and they had one darling infant, their firstborn child. In addition to their jobs, they had started a side business, one of those multilevel marketing plans. We thought they were just coming for coffee and dessert, but it soon became apparent that they were trying to rope us into this business venture.

As I realized what this couple sipping coffee and eating apple crisp in my home was up to, I began to feel bitter and judgmental. Their sales pitch was annoying and presumptuous. Besides that, their house was way nicer and much newer than ours. Her clothes were from a high-end store while I frequented resale shops or occasionally the sale rack at the department store. Of course, their two cars were also much nicer than the old Volkswagen Rabbit my husband and I shared.

I'll admit it. I was jealous. And I was rather self-righteous about my lifestyle choice when it came to being a stay-at-home mother. And so, when the conversation got around to women working outside the home, I chimed in.

"Oh, I am so grateful I get to be home with Mackenzie and

Mitchell. I'd rather live on bread and water than have someone else raising my kids."

Yes. I said that!

As I spoke, I saw the woman's countenance fall. She felt just horrible, I'm sure. However, I justified my words by thinking she needed to be convicted about her job choice — and it was my job to convict her (no Holy Spirit needed!). I am so ashamed now when I think back on that interaction.

If you want to be purely technical about it, the words I said were in fact true. I *was* grateful to be a stay-at-home mom. I *would* have eaten bread and water rather than give up my stay-at-home mom status. (Now, however, I am not so dogmatic about the whole stay-at-home mom versus working mother issue. I have met and am close friends with so many working moms who do a fabulous job raising their children. But back then? I thought staying home was not only the best, but also the only way!)

What I said was not untrue. The problem was why and how I said what I did. I said it in order to elevate myself. To make her look bad — and feel bad. I said it in a backhanded manner in order to make it obvious that I was choosing the nobler path while she was "neglecting her kid." And all of this because I was some combination of annoyed and jealous. This, my dear friends, was nothing short of sin. Yes, it is possible to speak words that pass the truth test, but to say them for totally wicked and selfish reasons, and in a manner designed to sting. Yes, when it comes to our words, motives and manners *do* matter.

If we want to become people who not only utter words that are true but also say them for the right reasons, what are we to do? How do we train our brains and tame our tongues in order to make sure that our motives and manners line up with God's Word? Whenever I need practical wisdom like this, one of the first places I look for answers is the book of Proverbs.

Examine Your Motives

As I mentioned earlier, I like to think of the book of Proverbs as the Twitter of the Old Testament. Such snappy sayings and crisp quotes! Every verse is written to make us wise. And they're so quotable — short snippets perfect for tweeting. Spending time both reading and memorizing verses from Proverbs is a practical step anyone can take to tame the tongue. When I peruse Proverbs for insights on why motives matter, three telling tweets ping off the page. They tell us what to watch for, a trick of the tongue to beware of, and a heart procedure we all probably need.

1. Watch for Blind Spots

Perhaps one of the most challenging things about examining motives is that we can't always see them for what they are — we have blind spots. If I rely only on my rearview mirror and don't turn my head to double check my car's blind spot, I may cause a crash injuring others and perhaps also myself. The same is true for my words. Consider this wise but painful insight:

All a person's ways seem pure to them,
   but motives are weighed by the LORD.
   (Proverbs 16:2)

Ouch. Here's raw biblical truth that affirms we can be flat-out self-deceived about the purity of own motives. We justify and explain. We offer excuses. We make an airtight case for why what we said was said in love. But the one thing we can't do? We can't fool God. He knows our true colors. Knowing that God knows us better than we know ourselves and sees our true motives should both keep us humble and make us careful. Because eventually we will have to answer on the day of judgment for every careless word we have spoken (Matthew 12:36). Yes, my sins and slips of the tongue will be wiped away by Jesus, but I'd rather not be reminded of a long list of them in my life review!

So if we think we are doing the right thing, but we are in fact blind to our motives, what are we to do? How can we see what God so clearly sees? We humbly ask for God's help, and then we do some serious and prayerful self-reflection. Here are a few questions to consider as you examine your motives before you speak.

> *Am I certain that what I want to say is true?* If so, then perhaps you should say it. But before you do, consider the remaining questions.
>
> *Is my goal to have my comment help the person or situation at hand? Or is it to put a little pinch in their heart?*
>
> *Do I feel my words will bring a solution or, if I'm totally honest, might they cause more of a problem?*
>
> *Even if what I plan to say is truthful, is my aim to say something that will make me look better by comparison?*
>
> *Have I earned the right to speak to this particular person?* If not, you should probably keep your lips zipped.
>
> *If I were speaking about this person to someone else, would I say the exact same thing as I would if that person were sitting in front of me?*
>
> *Are these words really necessary? Why?*
>
> *Have I prayed about it, or only thought about it in an effort to plan what I've already determined to say?*
>
> *Am I trying to play Holy Spirit and convict someone or guilt them into changing their mind?*
>
> *If the roles were reversed, would I want the other person to say the same thing to me?*

Once you have considered your blind spots and examined your motives carefully, then speak up if that is what the Lord is inviting you to do. For as Proverbs 16:23 says, "The hearts of the wise make their mouths prudent, and their lips promote instruction." Keeping your heart pure keeps your lips in line, and not only that — it makes what you *do* say instructive and helpful.

PROVERBS' TOP TEN
"TWEETS" ON THE TONGUE

Here are ten great tongue-tempering "tweets" from Proverbs you can memorize, scribble on a sticky note, or use as a screen saver on your cell phone.

Don't let your mouth speak dishonestly,
     and don't let your lips talk deviously. (4:24 HCSB)

The wise store up knowledge,
     but the mouth of a fool invites ruin. (10:14)

Evildoers are trapped by their sinful talk,
     and so the innocent escape trouble. (12:13)

The Lord detests lying lips,
     but he delights in people who are trustworthy. (12:22)

Those who guard their lips preserve their lives,
     but those who speak rashly will come to ruin. (13:3)

The mouths of fools are their undoing,
     and their lips are a snare to their very lives. (18:7)

A gossip betrays a confidence;
     so avoid anyone who talks too much. (20:19)

Watch your tongue and keep your mouth shut,
     and you will stay out of trouble. (21:23 NLT)

A lying tongue hates those it hurts,
  and a flattering mouth works ruin. (26:28)

Do you see someone who speaks in haste?
  There is more hope for a fool than for them. (29:20)

2. Beware the Sly Tongue

We can be blind to our motives, but that's not where the trouble ends. As we learn to discern the truth about what drives our speech, we need to beware of one more danger the writer of Proverbs warns about: "Like a north wind that brings unexpected rain is a sly tongue — which provokes a horrified look" (25:23).

According to the Merriam-Webster dictionary, the word *sly* means "clever in concealing one's aims or ends. Lacking in straightforwardness and candor. Lightly mischievous." Oh, how often my words have been just that! Quicker than lightning, my lips can string together a series of words that appear to mean one thing when in fact the exact opposite is true. In doing so, I "cleverly conceal my aim." Other times, I am sly simply by not being straightforward. I am trying to conceal my real feelings, so I speak in vague or misleading terms. Any time I find myself engaging in sly maneuvers, it's a signal that I need to stop and examine my motives. Why am I not being straightforward? Is there something I am trying to hide? If so, what is it, and why do I want to keep it hidden?

Then there's that aspect of *sly* defined as being *lightly* mischievous. The word *lightly* sheds a whole new light on the topic of mischievousness. It's not like I am trying to be all-out dishonest or disruptive. I am only slightly off course. Just a tiny bit dishonest or a tad bit mischievous. But as I often tell my children, a half-truth is still a whole lie. And a slam, whether overt or subtle, is still a slam.

And we can't ignore that part of the Proverbs verse about how a sly tongue provokes a horrified look from others. In other words, we may think we are clever and cunning or perhaps even entertaining with our verbal sleight of hand, but our misleading speech is often all too obvious to others — and shockingly so. When faced with the temptation to be sly — to hide behind our words or use them to mislead others — we need to push the pause button. Exploring the reasons for sly speech can help us to dig down deeper into our motives and save ourselves — and others — potential embarrassment.

3. Allow God's Word to Shape Your Heart

What other guidance do we find about motives and words in Proverbs? What about this: "Stop listening to instruction, my son, and you will stray from the words of knowledge" (19:27). The takeaway here? When we fail to spend time ingesting God's Word, we often spill out words that are wrong. Or as Jesus put it, "The mouth speaks from the overflow of the heart" (Matthew 12:34 HCSB), and "a good person produces good things from the treasury of a good heart, and an evil person produces evil things from the treasury of an evil heart" (Matthew 12:35 NLT). Spending time in God's Word shapes our hearts — it keeps us on the path of knowledge, which includes knowing the truth behind our motives. It helps us to replace our ill will and wrong motives with the perfect will and words of God. Whenever we stop listening to God's words of instruction, we will no doubt stray from the best (and right) thing to say. Instead, our words will not be wise. Our motives will not be pure. We will be speaking off-the-cuff, revealing the hidden foolishness of our hearts.

This has been so true in my life. I have been snarky with the hubby. Made a backhanded comment to the in-law. Complained to the pastor, pointing out everything I thought was wrong in a situation but failing to acknowledge my own fault. Used sarcasm with a friend, trying to drive home a point, but instead driving a stake into her heart.

Whenever I think back to a time when my mouth has tripped me up or my words have gotten me into trouble, I see it was usually at a time when I had also neglected the discipline of reading, studying, and memorizing the truths of Scripture. Oh, I tried to have a quiet time each morning. Sometimes I actually was very consistent in that. But other times I was not. And as the years passed and I had more children and even more responsibilities, it seemed like time to read, study, and memorize Scripture was scarce to nonexistent. But there came a point when I was determined to make a change.

As a busy mother of three, I knew I was not going to be able to carve out an entire hour or even half hour a day for soaking in the truth of Scripture. When I looked over my schedule and responsibilities, I saw only slim slices of time — maybe I had a few minutes while waiting in the car-pool line or in the waiting room at the orthodontist office. Perhaps I could find fifteen minutes in the late afternoon while something was simmering on the stove and I was waiting for the kids to get home from the homeschool academy they attended once a week.

And so I came up with an idea. Even though I already owned a Bible, I invested in a few more. I got a pocket-sized one to keep in my purse for those times when I was a lady-in-waiting. I could snatch up those few minutes during my day to read the Bible, rather than twiddling my fingers or browsing the months-old magazines in the doctor's office.

I invested in a waterproof Bible. Yes, there is such a thing! I keep it in my kitchen next to the coffee pot. Whenever I am doing dishes I can flip it open to a chapter in Proverbs or Psalms and drink deeply of the words of life. I can take it to the beach or swimming pool. And during those rare times that I actually get to sit and soak in a bubble bath, I can also soak in the Word of God.

I also made use of an app on my smartphone that *speaks* the Bible to me. My husband is currently using this app to listen to the entire Bible in one year. He grew weary vowing each year that he would read through the entire Bible but then failing to achieve his goal. Now he listens to a chunk of Scripture each morning during his half-hour commute to work. It takes him about twenty minutes a day, and by the end of the year he will have listened to the entire Bible from Genesis to Revelation.

A Bible app such as this or even the Bible on CD is a wonderful tool. I can listen while taking a walk or exercising on an elliptical machine. Listen while folding laundry or ironing or painting a room. We love to listen to music. Even sweeter to the ears are the words of Scripture. Let's vow to never stop listening to biblical instruction and by doing so to keep ourselves from straying from God's wise way.

Mama Was Right: Mind Your Manners

My mother-in-law is a stickler for manners. Her five children were taught which fork to use at a fancy meal, not to take a bite of dessert until the hostess was seated, and always to hold open doors for others. These manners help her offspring to not only be proper, but thoughtful and kind as well.

Being intentional in weighing our motives and careful in expressing our thoughts is one side of the equation when it comes to using words well, but there's still more. What happens when words that sting are said but we're not the one who said them? How we respond when we are on the receiving end of painful comments — regardless of whether they're spoken with good intentions or wrong motives — is just as important as examining our motives.

Like Debra Barone on *Everybody Loves Raymond*, I too have a member of my extended family who says things that hurt me. Over the years, I have often found myself in tears at family get-togethers. I have had my mothering skills subtly slammed. My method of making lasagna called into question. While I haven't been chided for being a bad housekeeper, I have been called a clean freak and a show-off for keeping my home organized. And worst of all are the cutting remarks about my weight.

At my daughter's thirteenth birthday, we hosted a huge crowd with members present from both sides of our extended family. We gathered out on our back deck on a delightfully sunny May afternoon. There was mesquite-grilled chicken. And lemon-pepper blackened pork chops. I put out my famous cheesy potato casserole alongside a ruby-red stack of watermelon slices. Pink and purple streamers decorated the deck, and my daughter was in her glory seeing all the relatives gather to pay tribute to her becoming a teenager.

I let everyone else go through the food line first and made sure my two boys had all of their food and utensils and were settled at the picnic table ready to enjoy the birthday feast. I then went through the food line and, admittedly, piled my plate too high with all of the birthday foods. At the end of the line was an assortment of cheesecakes. Marble swirl. Caramel pecan. Raspberry white chocolate. And apple praline. Just as I placed a piece of cheesecake on my already mountainous pile of food, I heard this particular relative pipe up.

This person began speaking to another extended family member who had recently been diagnosed with diabetes and had dropped about thirty pounds. "Oh, Jerry [well, we'll call him Jerry here]. You look marvelous. How much weight have you lost? I tell you, you look like a teenager! That diabetes was the best thing that ever happened to you. You look fabulous!" Then, without missing a beat, this person turned to me and, in front of the crowd of people (about fifteen in all), boldly declared, "Hey, Karen. Maybe you should get diabetes."

Totally. Not. Kidding.

I was so embarrassed and hurt. Although I am normally a chatterbox, I had no words to speak. Somehow I muddled through the rest of the party and then later cried myself to sleep.

My relationship with this person continued to be strained over the years. Not only would they speak words to my face that were hurtful, but I also found out from other relatives that they often talked behind my back. And sometimes they clipped magazine articles about what they considered one of my shortcomings and popped them in the mail to me just to make a point.

Another relative once asserted to me that, although this person's words often came across as spiteful and caustic, they, like Marie Barone's, really were motivated by love. Perhaps not with their comments about how I cooked or cleaned or raised my children, but when it came to my weight, they did not want to see me die prematurely from a heart attack like an aunt of mine had at about my age. And I guess they felt that calling me out in public and making comments to me about it whenever they saw me was going to motivate me to make a life change before it was too late.

Still, I harbored grudges. I could find neither forgiveness nor kindness in my heart for this difficult relative.

But then came the day my daughter played the lead in the eighth-grade production at her homeschool academy. That year they did *The Hiding Place*, the story of Corrie ten Boom, a Dutch Christian who, along with other members of her family, helped hide Jews during the height of the Holocaust. Corrie and her sister Betsie were imprisoned for their actions, and Betsie died in the infamous Ravensbrück concentration camp.

At the end of the play, a riveting scene takes place well after the war in which Corrie was out on the speaking circuit talking about her experiences. She was telling others about the love of Christ, who offers forgiveness to all no matter what they have done. After one of her talks, an audience member approached her, and Corrie recognized him as a former prison guard from Ravensbrück.

This guard, known as The Snake, had been cruel beyond belief, stripping prisoners and making them parade naked in front of members of the opposite sex. He had withheld food and medicine and had actually cost Corrie's sister Betsie her very life. As the man approached her, Corrie felt hatred welling up in her heart. But the guard, after hearing Corrie's message, had come forward to ask for her forgiveness.

Stunned, Corrie couldn't answer for a moment. Although she had suffered such abuse at the hand of this person and obviously had ill feelings toward him, she remembered what she had been speaking on that night: the love and forgiveness of Jesus Christ. She then thought, "How could I not extend forgiveness to this one who had so cruelly mistreated me when Jesus offered me forgiveness for my sins, which were exactly what nailed him to the cross?" And so, this messenger of the gospel extended her hand in forgiveness to her former captor.

As I sat in the dark auditorium that spring evening watching my daughter portray this amazing woman, I had this thought: *How could Corrie ten Boom forgive someone who treated her so brutally and even cost her sister her life, when I can't seem to forgive a family member who slams my domestic skills or makes an occasional crack about my weight?* With tears streaming down my face, I decided that my unforgiveness was holding me in a prison too. Of course it wasn't a physical place, but it was an awful place in my mind. There is truth to the old saying, "Unforgiveness is like sipping on poison and then expecting the other person to die." I knew this kind of poison could no longer be my beverage of choice.

I chose to forgive this relative — and to continue forgiving them whenever they made comments in the future. This doesn't mean I lie down as a doormat. Quite the opposite. In fact, my husband and I have put some boundaries in place when it comes to this person. I don't ever spend time with them alone since that seems to be the prime time when the cutting comments fly. Of course there are times, like at my daughter's birthday party, when they comment in front of others. At times like this we have decided we will leave quietly (or ask them to leave if they are at our home). We make it clear that, although we are leaving the premises, we are not leaving the relationship. We still love my relative, but we won't tolerate this behavior. I will, however, forgive the behavior. Because Jesus calls me to. And because I don't like the taste of poison.

Tough Skinned and Tenderhearted

It may seem like conflicting advice to be so careful with our own motives and manners but willingly forgive the misplaced or questionable motives and manners of others. But I have learned that this is the best place to park our minds. We must be diligent to weigh our own hearts and actions but give grace to others who speak ill of us.

Lysa TerKeurst is the president at Proverbs 31 Ministries, the organization for which I write and speak. She drew up a wonderful guideline for all of us as we interact with each other doing ministry together. When dealing with others, she declares, we should believe the best before we assume the worst. So when a conflict arises or our feathers get ruffled, we shouldn't automatically jump to the conclusion that the other person meant us ill, but give them the benefit of the doubt. Not assume the worst, but believe the best about their motives.

I liken this to a phrase my pastor often used when I was a teenager. He said that most people tend to have hard hearts and thin skins, but we as followers of Jesus should be different. Instead, we should be tenderhearted and tough skinned. Such wonderful advice. When we harden our hearts and let every little offense poke a hole in our happiness, we only hurt ourselves. We are slurping on a smoothie of poison, and we don't even know it. But when we soften our hearts with love for others, and toughen our skins against their barbs, we are better equipped to show the compassionate love of Jesus to a watching world.

Yes, believe the best. Don't assume the worst. And when it comes to your own words, check your motives and your manners before you engage your mouth.

When to Be Quiet

I will have many occasions to open my mouth in the days ahead. But before I engage my lips I must know with absolute certainty that what I am saying is true.

If I know for sure that something is not the truth, I need to be quiet.

If I have a strong hunch that something is not the truth, I need to be quiet.

If I have even the slightest doubt that something might not be true, I need to be quiet.

But just because something is true does not mean I always need to say it. Motives and manners matter. And so?

If something is true but saying it to someone will needlessly hurt their feelings, I need to be quiet. (Notice I didn't say I need to lie and tell them something they want to hear! No, I need to say nothing.)

If something is true but I know that my reason for saying it is to belittle someone or make them feel guilty, I need to be quiet.

If something is true but I promised to hold it in confidence, I need to be quiet.

If something is true but I know that my reason for saying it is to cause a rift between two people, I need to be quiet.

If something is true but my motive for speaking the truth is to make myself look better by comparison, I need to be quiet.

If something is true and I just feel in my heart that saying it will do nothing but make me feel good, in a sinister sort of way, I need to be quiet.

Bottom line? More often than not, I need to learn to keep it shut. How about you?

I think I have enough duct tape for the both of us.

6

BEHIND
THE SCREEN

Controlling Your Digital Tongue

If you play the fool and exalt yourself, or if you plan evil,
clap your hand over your mouth!

PROVERBS 30:32

I still remember the day I got a Facebook page back in 2007. I am pretty much a foreigner in the land of all things techie, but my kids insisted one day that I just could not be a cool mom unless I had a Facebook page. And so I let them create one for me.

Within hours, I had all kinds of requests to be "friends" with people. Some of them I knew in real life. A few were relatives. Some were even friends from way back in my high school or college days. But there were a few I had never even heard of. I wasn't sure how all of this had happened, and so I asked my kids. It turns out that they checked the box that automatically invited everyone I had ever emailed to be my "friend." In addition to friends and family, it also included all the random people I had emailed for one reason or another in the past. Event coordinators from churches where I'd spoken. Homeschool moms who were on an email newsletter group for my kids' co-op classes. For crying out loud, there were even people I had emailed from Craigslist because they wanted to buy my nightstand or I wanted to buy their used Ping-Pong table!

It amazed me that all of a sudden at the end of my fingertips was a whole new group of people I could talk with every day. And the group was so diverse! Before Facebook, I only occasionally ran into someone from my high school, but now I could hear from them weekly, see what they were doing, and even look at photographs of their children. I was grateful to connect with many of the friends from the Christian college I had attended, and it was a delight for me to see where they all were now. Facebook became a useful tool when connecting with my extended family, especially when coordinating who would bring what to Easter dinner.

At first, Facebook was fun. But then one day as I walked past the den, I heard my daughter hollering at the computer screen. "What? Are you kidding me right now? She is such a liar!"

I popped my head into the room to inquire about what had upset my daughter so much. She invited me to look at her friend's Facebook page. They were both members of a sports team, and a third girl, also a member, was on her friend's page complaining about the team's coach. The situation revolved around a kerfuffle this student had with the coach. One girl was on the side of the student. The other was on the side of the coach. The comments back and forth became sharper and more concerning. Pretty soon they were in an all-out Facebook fight, and other members of the team were hopping on to give their two cents' worth. At one point, a girl even used profanity. I couldn't believe my eyes.

I told my daughter to take down any comments she had made during this whole exchange, even though none of hers were inappropriate. I did not think a Facebook page was the place to settle an argument. Instead, the girls needed to talk as a team with their coach present, which is what they finally did at the next practice.

Snark Rules on Social Media

This whole age of social media is still slightly foreign to me. It just strikes me as strange that friends can argue online or complete strangers can engage in a hearty debate right there on my blinking screen for all the world to see. Back in my high school days, if we had an issue with someone, we talked to them. Or I guess sometimes we did write a note to a friend. But usually our fights were not a public fireworks display. And don't even get me started on bullying. The worst we had to worry about was a nasty note getting passed around school. Now kids are bullied online to the point of tragic consequences.

Although the Bible was written long before the computer age, I am convinced the truths of Scripture that address how we use our words in speech applies equally to how we use our words in cyberspace. In fact, sometimes it's the online words that give us the most trouble.

There is just something empowering about saying what you really think while hiding behind a computer screen. Maybe we feel courageous because the person we're addressing isn't physically present. Or perhaps peer pressure and going along with the crowd makes it easy to speak harshly. Whatever it is, I have witnessed many people say things in cyberspace I doubt they would ever say in person. Sometimes the keyboard really does bring out the worst in us.

In a little survey I did with over five hundred of my blog readers, I discovered some interesting statistics about communicating online. Over half of those in the survey, 52 percent, admitted saying something online they know they would never have said in person. Almost 15 percent indicated that they had done this more than a dozen times. And when it came to the question about whether they had seen someone else say something online that they were pretty sure the person would never say to someone's face, 100 percent of them had witnessed such a scenario.

Social media has become a playground for loud opinion slinging. Snark rules the day, and caustic comments are the norm. Even now as I just grabbed my smartphone and scrolled through my Twitter account, I read comments from three different people picking a fight, one making an argument against what a friend had said, and two women in an all-out war harassing a third woman for a Bible verse she put up that they think is ridiculous since they do not believe in the existence of God.

Facebook and Twitter are not the only breeding grounds for cutting comments and fight picking. I have seen it on Instagram too. Now Instagram happens to be my favorite choice of social media. I love seeing pictures my daughter posts as well as those from friends and family. Somehow I thought that a venue to just share photos would be a safe place with kind comments only. Boy, was I wrong! People are just as likely to flame (post hostile and derisive comments) on Instagram as on any other social media outlet.

One of my friends also happens to be famous. She has made television shows and movies, and I'm sure if I dropped her name you would recognize her. But trust me, she is also a lightning rod for negative comments. This friend has an Instragram account. As a Christian in Hollywood, she gets vicious criticism for posting any picture that has to do with God, the Bible, or church. A quick scroll through her dozens, sometimes hundreds, of comments reveals many people slamming her for her faith. I've often wondered just why these people follow her on Instagram in the first place if they cannot stomach her or what she stands for. Go figure.

At the other end of the spectrum, there are Christians who also slam her even though she is one of them, when she doesn't practice her faith in the ways they think she should.

One day she posted a picture of some cute new shoes she was wearing. She wrote something like, "Thanks, [name of the shoe brand] for these darling flats. Now I feel like it is summer!" A few people made very sweet and encouraging comments about how darling the shoes were or how happy they were that summer was finally here too. But it just took one brave soul to start a comment chain of criticism. This person had looked up the exact shoes online to find out the price. Then she made a comment telling everyone how much the shoes cost and chastising my friend for buying what she deemed was an excessively expensive pair of shoes when there are starving children in the world and missionaries who need money. Pretty soon other women began piling on like a free-for-all fight in a hockey rink:

"How dare you!"

"I could never afford those shoes. Must be nice to be rich."

"Seriously? You mean you can't buy shoes at Walmart like the rest of us?"

"Do you know how many starving children you could've fed for that amount of money?"

And on it went.

What I found interesting, and almost a little humorous, was that my friend's original comment when she posted the picture revealed that she had gotten the shoes for free. Sure enough, the shoe company had sent her a complimentary pair. She hadn't paid a penny for them. Someone eventually posted this fact in the comment thread, which helped to shut down the Christian critics at least.

What I found saddest is that I know my friend gives tons of money to her church and to charities. She is a generous and godly woman who takes a lot of heat for her faith. I'm certain that none of the women who criticized her actually know her in real life. I'm not even sure why they follow her on Instagram, because no matter what she posts they have something negative to say about it.

All of this opinion slinging and fight picking on social media brings to mind more wise words from Proverbs: "As charcoal to embers and as wood to fire, so is a quarrelsome person for kindling strife" (26:21). Cutting and accusatory comments can fan the flames of debate and argument, inviting others to throw more wood on the fire. The embers smolder, and the flickering flames grow higher. Before long, a blaze of strife rages right before our very eyes. When a quarrelsome person publicly vents for all the world to see, it empowers others to also use their digital tongues in a detrimental way. We must be careful to stay away from these destructive fires.

Blog Blather

I have a blog. I have many friends who also are bloggers. It never ceases to amaze me how many people seem to actually enjoy leaving critical, combative, or very "holier than thou" comments on a blog. I have come to expect this if the blog post is about something controversial. Many Christians have strong opinions, especially on spiritual matters. Issues like whether infant baptism is okay or if it must be only adults who are baptized. Or the method of baptism. Sprinkle or dunk? Is only one way correct, or are both allowed? These exchanges over hot-button aspects of the Christian faith have been debated throughout the centuries. I guess it should come as no humongous surprise that believers drag these controversies into the age of social media and continue to have hearty debates over them.

My blog has a tagline that declares its mission: "Live your priorities. Love your life." I like to equip women with doable ideas and simple tools that will help them to live their priorities. Their relationship with God. Their marriage and mothering. And their interaction with others. So sometimes I write about marriage or mothering. Other days I talk about getting your house organized. And often, I might share a recipe. Nothing controversial about a recipe, right? Oh my . . .

One day I posted a vegetarian main dish recipe. However, it needed a little bit of broth in it, and so I stated this. In parentheses I put "chicken or beef bouillon cubes," assuming if someone were a vegetarian, they would use vegetable broth. I only added in the other two options for those people who did not have vegetable broth on hand but most likely would have a beef or chicken bouillon cube in their pantry.

One woman hopped right on and commented that she was appalled I would bill a recipe as vegetarian and then have the gall to suggest adding chicken or bouillon cubes. She was very angry. I tried to explain that of course vegetable broth would be used for an all-vegetarian version, and assured her I was only trying to offer an option.

Apparently, my explanation did not satisfy her. She continued to hammer me publicly and shame me for what I had done. I ended up deleting her comments because I couldn't see the sense in a simple recipe sparking a war of "carnivore versus vegetarian."

Another time I put up what I thought was a humorous comment on my Facebook page on a Friday evening during

Lent. My son had invited over several members of the football team for dinner that night. I made spaghetti and meatballs and thought it was rather strange that a couple of his friends took only salad and vegetables. Then I realized what was happening. I wrote this on my Facebook page: "Note to self: When hosting a Friday night dinner for my son's friends during Lent, it might be best to pass up making meatballs. Oops! Shoulda gone for the fish sticks."

Oh, boy, did that ever spark a debate reminiscent of the Reformation! One woman hopped on and urged me to sit those Catholic boys down and explain to them that they can eat all the fish sticks they want and it won't get them into heaven. A few more lamented over their Catholic upbringing and how they hated eating fish on Fridays. Some who were Catholic defended their faith as the only authentic Christian tradition. Back and forth the heated opinions were slung — all stemming from what I intended to be a simple statement about my own oversight!

Although I'm not Catholic, I was actually very proud of these two boys. They were not only upholding a practice of their faith, they were doing so when their parents weren't around. They could easily have chowed down on some meatballs without Mom and Dad ever knowing. I commended them for sticking to their Lenten commitment and made them peanut butter and jelly sandwiches instead. And it broke my heart to see the mud-slinging between the Catholics and Protestants. So very sad. I want my Facebook page to be a welcoming place. I am not interested in allowing it to be a forum for needless fights and debates.

Rules for the Cyberspace Playground

If we want to honor God with what we say on the cyberspace playground, what are the guidelines we should follow? Here's more pithy advice from Proverbs: "If you play the fool and exalt yourself, or if you plan evil, clap your hand over your mouth!" (30:32). Here it is, translated for social media: "If you are tempted to slam someone online or brag on Facebook or send off a nasty tweet, *turn off the screen and walk away!*"

That's it in a nutshell, but maybe we should spell out some rules of thumb that might keep our thumbs and fingers from wandering off into slander, arrogance, or combativeness. Here are six that work for me.

1. Pray Before You Post

My friend Suzanne wrote a great online devotional in which she talked about how many people run to check their Facebook page first thing in the morning. She encouraged her readers to instead make sure they consulted their "Faithbook" first — the Bible. How true this is! Perhaps if we spent time ingesting words of truth before we switched on the computer, we might not write things that are unkind or hurtful. At the very least, we should whisper a prayer before we post, asking the Holy Spirit to tap on our hearts if we are tempted to post anything online that would not glorify him.

2. Imagine the Recipient Sitting Next to You

The Internet is so impersonal. We see tiny little thumbnail photos of people. We see words typed out on a screen rather than hear them spoken out loud. The pixels-and-pictures environment almost compels us to be rude because it lacks the subtle social cues — the wince, the moment of quiet — that tell us we've crossed the line. We feel empowered and also have a sense of anonymity as we tap, tap, tap away on our keyboards. But if a flesh-and-blood person were sitting next to us with eyes we could look into, perhaps we would state things differently. Before you post, ask yourself if you would say things differently if the person to whom you're writing were actually sitting next to you.

3. Remember: When You're Online, You're Also on Stage

Unless we send a private message, our online words are available for others to see. Twitter followers see what we tweet. Facebook friends, and the friends of those on whose walls we post comments, also see what we say. And hundreds, if not hundreds of thousands, of people can see a comment we leave on someone's blog. This reality should certainly cause us to pause before we post — especially if there is even a remote possibility we might later regret what we write. If I say something in person to a friend and am later convicted I was wrong, I can go back to my friend and apologize. However, if I post something on social media or comment on a blog and later want to retract it, I have no way to chase down all of the people who might have seen the original comment. Just this fact alone should cause us to really weigh our words before we type them out.

4. Ask Yourself If You've Earned the Right to Address the Subject at Hand

If friends on Facebook are hashing through a hot-button issue of the day, do you have any expertise in the area, or are you only slinging an underinformed opinion? We can't always be an expert on every topic at hand, so when we aren't, we might do well to refrain from commenting at all.

5. Ask Yourself If You Have a Close Enough Relationship with the Person to Warrant Offering Your Opinion

It both irks me and makes me laugh when I see who hops on my page to offer their unsolicited opinions. Suddenly, people I haven't heard from in years pop up on my screen offering their pixelated opinion about something I've posted. They give me specific instructions and pointed advice on what I should believe about a particular topic. This always surprises me because I don't have a close relationship with these folks. Why do they think I will take their advice or value their perspective on my issues when they have not been a close friend or confidant? Would they be responsive to unsolicited advice if someone they knew years ago suddenly walked up to them on the street and started telling them what to believe and how to act?

If you're tempted to dole out unsolicited advice to anyone who's not a trusted friend, then I encourage you to resist the temptation!

6. When You Do Speak, Let Your Speech Be Laced with Grace

No need for snark. No need for angry words or critical comments. Our mamas were right: If we can't say something nice, we shouldn't say anything at all. When we do speak, we can choose to be gracious rather than accusatory or negative. Our words must glorify God and not just exalt our own opinions. We should be especially mindful that there are people whom we don't know who might be viewing our online speech. Here is a great guideline from Scripture: "Be wise in the way you act toward outsiders; make the most of every opportunity. Let your conversation be always full of grace, seasoned with salt, so that you may know how to answer everyone" (Colossians 4:5–6).

So maybe we should jot down these questions on a sticky note or two and post them near the computer to remind us to ask:

- Is this comment wise?
- Will writing this comment help me display God's love to outsiders?
- Is this comment full of grace?

- Is this comment seasoned with salt?

- Have I asked God if this is the best response?

Most of those questions are pretty straightforward. But what does the Bible mean by seasoned with salt? Let's take a closer look and find out.

Salty Speech

In high school, my pastor did a message series on the Sermon on the Mount. At one point Jesus states: "You are the salt of the earth. But if the salt loses its saltiness, how can it be made salty again? It is no longer good for anything, except to be thrown out and trampled underfoot" (Matthew 5:13). My pastor devoted an entire message to explaining what being "the salt of the earth" meant. I had never considered the many uses of salt, especially in the ancient world of Jesus' day. So when I did a little research, I discovered even more about the many uses and significance of salt.

Salt Enhances Flavor

Salt is the number one flavor enhancer in the world. People sprinkle it on their corncobs, shake it on piping hot french fries, and add a dash to steaming bowls of soup. Salt is even sometimes put on sweet things to intensify their sweetness. My father always puts it on his watermelon or cantaloupe. The barista at my local coffeehouse cracks some sea salt on top of caramel hot cocoa and its mounds of whipped cream. And have you ever tasted dark chocolate with sea salt? Oh. My. Word.

Most traditional baked dessert recipes include salt. One time I forgot to add salt to a mint brownie recipe. When I tasted it I could tell something was wrong. There was plenty of mint and cocoa powder, the two main flavors of the dish, but somehow it just didn't taste right. Even though the recipe called for only half a teaspoon, omitting the salt ruined the normally delicious treat. It takes only a little salt to coax out the wonderful flavor of other things around it.

When it comes to your words, are you adding flavor? Are you bringing out sweetness in both your choice of words and in conversation with others, especially online conversations? Will you purpose to add the flavor of Christ instead of adding not just bland but maybe even *bad* ingredients? Do your words add flavor?

Salt Preserves

I grew up with a mother and grandmother who did a lot of home canning. As a result, I also can a lot of produce each summer. Pickles. Stewed tomatoes. Apple butter. Salsa. And my famous corn relish. Common to all of these diverse food items is one ingredient: salt.

Salt has always been used as a preservative. It helps to cure meat, keeping it from spoiling. When sailors in the nineteenth and early twentieth centuries had to be out at sea for months, they existed on a diet of mostly salt-cured meats. While untreated meat will last only a day or so without refrigeration, meat preserved with salt can last with no refrigeration for three to four months.

Every day, we see evidence of a society decaying all around us. If you don't see it, perhaps you haven't been on the Internet lately. And I'm not just talking about immoral and disturbing websites; it's evident in all the hateful and thoughtless comments we read on every form of social media. As Christians, we have to ask ourselves, do our words add to the decay? We are called to be the salt of the earth. Our words can help preserve the truth of God as we interact with others, in person and online.

When you comment online, are you humbly and gently speaking truth, preserving the very words of God as you do so?

Salt Is Valuable

Have you ever heard the phrase "Worth his weight in salt"? In generations past, salt was often used as currency. Because it was so essential for flavoring and preserving, it was a valuable commodity. People traded goods in exchange for salt. Salt throughout the ages has been very valuable.

Do your words online add value to the conversation at hand?

Salt Purifies and Softens

When we lived in a house out in the country, we had what is commonly referred to as "hard water" because it had a very high mineral content. Before we treated the problem, our shower stall turned a light shade of rusty orange. The minerals also built up in the showerhead, eventually making it difficult for the water to get out. And I had to work hard to scrub the mineral deposits off the walls of the shower and out of the bottom of the sinks.

Then we got a water softener. Every so often we filled up the chamber of the softener with salt pellets. The salt pellets served two purposes: they softened the water by filtering out minerals that were causing a gunky buildup, and they prohibited the growth of bacteria in the water, helping to purify it.

When it comes to your speech, are you exhibiting these properties of salt? Are your words soft? Are they pure? Or are they harsh and impure?

Salt Melts Hard Ice

Living in the Midwest for my entire life, I have seen many harsh winters. In fact, we are just coming out of one of the worst winters in the past eighty years. We had many subzero days, with windchills sometimes twenty or thirty degrees below zero. And of course we had snow. Lots of snow. In one forty-eight hour stretch, over eighteen inches of snow fell. And just a few days before Christmas we witnessed one of the worst ice storms of the century. Ice more than an inch thick encased trees and power lines, many of which came crashing down, knocking out electricity for nearly a week.

With all this ice and snow every winter, my state of Michigan has to be well equipped with plows and salt trucks. After every storm, workers plow the snow and salt the roads to melt the ice. We also buy bags of salt to sprinkle on our own sidewalks and porches to melt the hard ice that forms there.

People can be cold. Icy cold. When you interact with them, do your words help to melt the ice or add to the chilly climate? If you are given the cold shoulder, do you give it right back, or do you try to warm things up a bit by gently and respectfully engaging them with kindhearted dialog? When your words are carefully seasoned with salt, they may melt the iciest of hearts.

Salt Prevents Infection in a Wound

In the ancient world of Jesus' day, salt was often sprinkled on a wound to keep it from getting infected. Salt halted the spread of infection that could make the laceration increasingly more painful and cause it to take longer to heal. Sure, the salt stung for a moment, but it could also save the injured person's life if it prevented a runaway infection.

At those times when we encounter gossip and rumors, we can choose to halt the spreading of the infectious words or scandalous stories by refusing to participate. And if we are brave enough to speak up and declare that we don't want to hear — and certainly don't care to repeat — what is being said, like salt, our words may sting for a moment, but our actions may help to squelch a rumor and stop the gossip before it spreads, infecting others and causing more pain.

Will you bravely speak up in an attempt to stop the spread of infectious speech before it causes even more pain? Or will you utilize silence — refusing to participate in a gossip session — and help to halt the destructive dialog that is happening?

Too Much Salt Destroys the Dish

We've talked a lot about watching our words online. About making sure they don't start, or even escalate, a fight. About how our words should be soft. And pure. They should add value to the conversation and be flavored with the character of Christ. But sometimes, a Christian can overdo the salt.

Sometimes we may be called upon to speak the truth as it is found in Scripture. In those moments, remember that a little salt goes a long way. Answer with gentleness and respect. Keep your comments brief and humble. Carefully tailor your words to the situation and person at hand, rather than dumping the contents of your saltshaker all over the place. Remember, too much salt not only destroys the dish, but can also sour a relationship.

Will you choose to keep your comments truthful yet tight so as not to preach or condemn, coming off holier-than-thou?

Common table salt. Sodium chloride. NaCl on the periodic table. How many uses there have been through the ages! Salty speech is crucial if we want to be like Jesus. But please — don't let the many uses of salt and the spiritual parallels overwhelm you. Maybe try to work on one or two areas at a time. As you reflect on the many uses of salt, do so with an attitude of prayer. Ask the Lord to reveal which characteristic of salty speech you most need to work on in the days ahead.

Using Your Digital Tongue Wisely

No doubt this week, perhaps even today, you will have an opportunity to use your digital tongue. Maybe you will tweet. Or hop on Facebook to chime in on a conversation. Perhaps you will leave comments on a blog. When you do, what kind of words will you use?

Here is a little challenge from Scripture to help us keep our tongues in check:

> My mouth speaks what is true,
>> for my lips detest wickedness.
> All the words of my mouth are just;
>> none of them is crooked or perverse. (Proverbs 8:7–8)

Yes, this is a high standard. But I say we should shoot for it. There is an old saying, "If you aim for nothing, you will hit it every time." Let's not be aimless when it comes to our online words. Let's seek to make them pleasing to God and encouraging to those who read them.

7 BUT I'M JUST SHARING A PRAYER REQUEST

Stopping Gossip and Hearsay

So live that you would not mind selling
your pet parrot to the town gossip.

WILL ROGERS

I loved Saturday nights when I was a child. Since church and Sunday school were the next morning, Saturday night was the time to take a bubble bath. My mom filled the tub and poured in the pink bubble bath the nice Avon lady had brought to our house. I soaked and played with the bubbles, piling them high on top of my head or crafting a long Santa Claus beard for myself. When the bubbles started to pop and wane, I poured more bubble bath under the running faucet to make them rise high again.

When it came time for shampooing, I leaned back, dipping my wavy, blond, waist-length mane into the water. After soaping it up with my No More Tears shampoo (Improperly named in my opinion. That stuff always made my eyes water!), my mom rinsed my hair with a big plastic cup full of clear warm water.

Once I was dried off and buttoned into my flannel nightgown, mom rolled up my hair in spongy pink curlers. Then I curled up on the living-room sofa in my scratchy pink bathrobe, waiting for my favorite TV show to come on. The show was the country music variety show *Hee Haw*. And I couldn't get enough of it.

The hilarious antics of the country folk in fictional Kornfield Kounty always made me laugh. And my dad laughed even louder. He got a kick out of all of the pickin' and grinnin' going on as well as the recurring characters on the show. Like the suspenders-clad old man to whom the crowd would pose the question, "Hey, Grandpa! What's for supper?" He'd answer in rhyme, describing a crazy country supper full of corn bread and collard greens. But the one recurring skit I loved most was where a bunch of girls, washing clothes by hand and playing musical instruments, would sing the following little ditty:

Now, we're not ones to go around spreadin' rumors.
Why, really we're just not the gossipy kind.
Oh, you'll never hear one of us repeating gossip.
So you'd better be sure and listen close the first time.

After this twangy opening verse was sung each week, the characters took turns telling a bit of recent news about someone in Kornfield Kounty. Although it was never anything too racy or scandalous, the details they told were still pure, juicy gossip. Spreading rumors was supposed to be something good girls didn't do, of course, but with a wink of the eye, these ladies let 'em fly.

Threads of Gossip

As I got older, I often felt a little bit like those *Hee Haw* honeys who strung together words in pure threads of gossip. Even though I knew I shouldn't be "talking behind someone's back,"

113

as my mama called it, sometimes I just couldn't help myself. While the ladies on that Saturday evening TV show got laughs from the audience, I got attention from my friends. I soon learned how to work my words in such a way that people wanted to hear me talk. And not only that. I also began to develop a love of *listening* to gossip as well. President Teddy Roosevelt's daughter Alice once declared, "If you haven't got anything nice to say about anybody, come sit next to me." That seemed to be my philosophy too. And living my life enjoying both speaking and listening to gossip got me into plenty of down-home trouble.

In addition to that time I got half of eighth grade angry at me for saying Bill Warner thought my friend Janet kissed like a fish, I had many other conflicts that originated with gossip that rolled off my tongue. Even though speaking or listening to gossip (and then repeating it to someone else) often landed me in hot water, I just couldn't stop. I was addicted to talking behind other people's backs and listening to others do the same. Gossip brought excitement to my life, almost giving me an adrenaline rush. Unfortunately, this bad habit carried on for years, even through college, causing me great heartache, pain, and wounded relationships. You'd think I would have learned my lesson early on, but I didn't. After falling to the ground and getting hurt, I just dusted myself off and hopped right back on the high horse of dirt dishing, riding off into yet another high-drama conflict.

Gossip had me in its grip.

Hearsay: A Slick Trick

Gossip is dangerous and destructive. But so is gossip's first cousin. His name is hearsay.

Hearsay is a slick little fellow. You can get away with this form of gossipy speech because it doesn't originate with you. It can't be traced back to you so sometimes you feel a little more empowered to spread hearsay around. Just the very word *hearsay* makes it seem as though it is something that you just "heard" someone else "say." Sometimes this is the case. More often it is a little squishier than that. With hearsay, we can't nail down just where the thoughts or accusations came from. It's just the "word on the street." A rumor. A report. Some talk. Something that came down through the grapevine.

Passing on hearsay is repeating something without verification. You could be passing on the truth or you could be spreading a lie. For most folks, deciding whether or not to pass along a bit of hearsay depends directly on whether or not you believe it, or whether or not you wish to do damage to someone. In fact, you may fully believe that bit of hearsay you have just encountered is not true, but it could be detrimental to the person it is being spoken about, whom you happen not to like. And so, sad to say, it gets passed on.

Another danger in fanning the fires of hearsay is the temptation to add on your own little thoughts and details to the skeleton of the unverified story. After all, if the original bit of information cannot be traced directly back to you, how will anyone know where it took on some additional flavor?

And here's where there is yet another danger unique to Christians. We engage in hearsay and justify it with a thin, Jesus-y glaze cloaked as a prayer request. Yes! That's it! We aren't repeating gossip or spreading a rumor, we are sharing a prayer request. And who could fault us for that? Especially if we seem genuinely concerned for the person. If confronted for talking about someone behind their back, we have an out, a just-trying-to-be-a-good-Christian escape hatch. It was just a prayer request.

Yes, hearsay is a slick little fellow.

An Ancient Problem

Gossip. Hearsay. Are these relatively recent problems in society? Nope. They were problems even in biblical times. In fact, as long as there have been more than two people on the planet, people have talked behind someone else's back.

> Jacob and his mother Rebekah plotted against his brother Esau to steal his birthright (Genesis 27).
> Joseph's brothers complained about him and connived with each other to cause him harm (Genesis 37).
> The people grumbled about Moses when he wasn't around (Exodus 16:2).
> Job's three friends had a powwow to discuss his troubles and then set out to "comfort" him (Job 2:11).
> David consulted with others in order to bring about the death of a man because he wanted that man's wife for his own (2 Samuel 11:15).
> People from his hometown talked amongst themselves about Jesus, wondering what was so great about him since he was just the carpenter's son (Matthew 13:55; Mark 6:3).
> The apostle Paul had to set some church folks straight when they talked about him in his absence (1 Corinthians 4:19).

Yes, our words about others have been a problem since the dawn of time.

Let's take a closer look at these forms of speech and try to discover some biblical insight that might help us the next time we are tempted to repeat something we've heard, say something behind someone's back we would never say to their face, or spread an untruth.

WHAT GOSSIP IS AND IS NOT

When we talk about the concept of gossip, does that mean we can't ever talk about another person when they are not present? I think the answer is no. It may sometimes be appropriate and necessary. So how do we differentiate between what is and is not gossip? Perhaps this checklist can help:

Gossip is when:

- We divulge a secret we were specifically asked not to share.

- We divulge a secret that we are pretty sure is not meant to be shared, even if we weren't explicitly instructed not to repeat it.

- We tell a story about someone we have not yet verified to be true.

- We speak about others in a way that paints them in a negative light so the listener will form an unflattering opinion.

- We talk in a cryptic way about someone, subtly suggesting something questionable or even scandalous about his or her character.

- We start out a story with a statement such as, "You know, they say …" "They" can speak for themselves. Quoting "they" as the source of a story is a red flag. "They" are the origin point of ginormous amounts of gossip.

Gossip is not:

- Processing a conflict or difficult situation between you and another person (or persons) with a trusted and tight-lipped friend, family member, mentor, counselor, or support group. The words spoken are straightforward facts, and you make no effort to cast the other person in a bad light. You truly desire support, guidance, and prayer for handling the situation.

- Giving your honest opinion when asked about someone's character in a reference situation, such as when someone is applying for a job, a scholarship, or a leadership position.

- Giving your opinion about another person with words that impart grace, point out the honorable parts of their personality and character, and leave the less-than-lovely parts unsaid. My mama always told me that if you look hard enough, you can find the good in anyone. This reminds me of an old rhyme that goes like this:

> There's so much good in the worst of us,
> and so much bad in the best of us,
> that it hardly becomes any of us,
> to talk about the rest of us.

Gossip in the Bible

The word *gossip* appears at least a dozen times in both the Old and New Testaments. The Old Testament Hebrew word is *rakil*, which refers to one who travels about speaking slander or telling tales. The New Testament Greek word is *psithurismos*, which describes a whisperer who goes around revealing secrets in order to paint someone else in a bad light. Throughout the Bible, a gossip is never spoken of highly. Gossip is always treated as something that does damage and is to be avoided.

Interestingly enough, the Bible rarely uses the word gossip as a verb. It is usually a noun. Today we often use *gossip* as a verb — an action word. "Now, don't talk like that. You're *gossiping*." Or, "She runs off her mouth constantly, *gossiping* all the time." But the Bible doesn't separate the act of gossip from the person who does it. Gossip is something one *is*. It is a label. A label that sticks. And stinks.

Let's look it at another way. Suppose you have a friend who really likes to sing but she's not particularly skilled at it. Yes, she may occasionally sing with the worship team at church or belt out a tune as she is driving along in her car, but she is just a person who happens to like singing. You wouldn't really characterize her as a singer.

But let's say another friend has a phenomenal singing voice. She is so good that she is paid to sing in public, and you are just sure if she could get up the nerve to compete, she would make the top ten on *American Idol*. (And you'd be right there in the first row of the audience cheering her on and hoping to meet Ryan Seacrest in person!) That friend of yours has earned the label of *singer*. Singing is something she does so well the word doesn't just describe what she *does*; it embodies who she *is*.

Those of us who have a habit of spreading untruths or saying unflattering things about people behind their backs earn the label *gossip*. And Scripture has some pretty strong words when it comes to such a person. We'll explore that and how to stop gossiping later in the chapter. For now let's look at the flip side — what it's like to be on the receiving end of gossip.

On the Receiving End

I doubt if there is a person alive who hasn't been a victim of gossip. So how should we respond when we discover we are being gossiped about?

Psalm 31 is a poem filled with raw emotion in which David both praises God and yet also laments the evil ways he has been treated — not just by his enemies but also his closest friends. The psalm begins with an appeal for God's help and protection:

> In you, LORD, I have taken refuge;
>   let me never be put to shame;
>   deliver me in your righteousness.
> Turn your ear to me,
>   come quickly to my rescue;
> be my rock of refuge,

> a strong fortress to save me.
> Since you are my rock and my fortress,
>   for the sake of your name lead and guide me.
> Keep me free from the trap that is set for me,
>   for you are my refuge.
> Into your hands I commit my spirit;
>   deliver me, LORD, my faithful God. (vv. 1–5)

David seems to have a pretty unwavering faith in God, knowing it is God alone who is his refuge. But he is also aware of the dangers lurking out there, which the psalm goes on to describe:

> I hate those who cling to worthless idols;
>   as for me, I trust in the LORD.
> I will be glad and rejoice in your love,
>   for you saw my affliction
>   and knew the anguish of my soul.
> You have not given me into the hands of the enemy
>   but have set my feet in a spacious place.
> Be merciful to me, LORD, for I am in distress;
>   my eyes grow weak with sorrow,
>   my soul and body with grief.
> My life is consumed by anguish
>   and my years by groaning;
> my strength fails because of my affliction,
>   and my bones grow weak.
> Because of all my enemies,
>   I am the utter contempt of my neighbors
> and an object of dread to my closest friends —
> those who see me on the street flee from me.
> I am forgotten as though I were dead;
>   I have become like broken pottery. (vv. 6–12)

And then we come to the gossip.

I have heard the gossip of many;
    terror is on every side.
When they conspired against me,
    they plotted to take my life. (v. 13 HCSB)

Here, the psalm takes a bit of a turn. In verses 14 through 16, David again affirms his trust in God. It's almost as if he's trying to convince himself that God really is in control. My friend Renee Swope calls this "bossing your heart around." It's a heart-rattling experience when other people use lies to come after us. At those times, repeating out loud the promises of God and remembering his power can help us to calm our anxious hearts. Or to quote Psalm 31:

How abundant are the good things
    that you have stored up for those who fear you,
that you bestow in the sight of all,
    on those who take refuge in you.
In the shelter of your presence you hide them
    from all human intrigues;
you keep them safe in your dwelling
    from accusing tongues. (vv. 19–20)

David gets his eyes off of the gossip and his enemies and puts them back on God. So often we are tempted to fix our eyes in the wrong place. Especially when we know others are talking about us, we can so easily obsess about what they might be saying.

During the time in eighth grade when I lost a lot of friends, I knew people were talking about me. I could see groups of girls huddled around a locker in the hallway laughing and talking as I approached. As I grew closer, their voices got quieter yet the looks on their faces displayed contempt. I knew notes about me were being passed around school. And one time a girl shouted over my head to another to call her later that afternoon. She then said she had new information about "you know who." The condescending look she shot my way left me no doubt about just who that "who" was.

Although I had brought the trouble on myself, the retaliatory gossip hurt me deeply. It was so very hard for me to concentrate on school or most anything else in life during this time. I was consumed with a feeling of dread. I climbed up the stairs of the yellow school bus each morning with a pit in my stomach. I couldn't wait for school to be over so I could go back home and flip on the TV to immerse myself in a sitcom and forget my troubles. But my troubles were a resilient thing. They kept bouncing back into the forefront of my thoughts. I simply couldn't find a distraction big enough to dislodge them.

Sensing something was awry, my mom asked me one day what was wrong. I relayed a condensed version of the story. She gave me a good pep talk, asserting that if girls were acting like that toward me, who wanted them as friends anyway? She went on to point out all the wonderful characteristics others saw in me and reassured me that I would soon make new friends. But one thing she said really stuck with me. She told me I should care more about what God thought about me than about what others did. I tried to keep that perspective as I went through my day, and it did help. Although at this point in my life I wasn't following God seriously, I did know enough about him to know that he was more powerful than all the wagging tongues at school.

This perspective of God as bigger than any circumstance is the one David takes in Psalm 31. The psalm wraps up with him no longer afraid of the accusing tongues, but tucked safely into God's dwelling place. He praises the Lord for the wonders of his love and for coming to his rescue when he cried out for help. He buttons up the entire piece with these words:

> Love the LORD, all his faithful people!
> The LORD preserves those who are true to him,
> but the proud he pays back in full.
> Be strong and take heart,
> all you who hope in the LORD. (vv. 23–24)

What is the takeaway of this emotion-packed psalm? Can we unearth any truth or action plans that we should implement today if we ourselves have been the victims of gossip?

Oh yeah. A few.

First …

1. Know Whose Words Provide Protection

(Psst … it isn't yours!)

In the New Living Translation, the first verse of Psalm 31 reads: "O LORD, I have come to you for protection; don't let me be disgraced."

I love it that right out of the chute, David runs to God rather than rushing to his own defense. He declares that God is the one who provides protection. This, I admit, is not my first inclination when I'm on the receiving end of gossip. When I know that someone thinks something about me that is not true, the first thing I want to do is start talking to anyone who will listen in order to protect my reputation. But protecting my reputation is not my job. It is God's. My job is to watch my words in the first place. My job is to run to God for protection rather than try to protect my fragile image.

My mentor in high school and college, the woman who first

helped me discover a relationship with God, used to tell me that all I needed to do at times like this was to be quiet and pray. To let the Lord fight for me while I rested in him. She quoted these words from the Old Testament: "The LORD will fight for you; you need only to be still" (Exodus 14:14). The best way I have learned over the years to be still is to dive into the pages of my Bible. Immersing myself in God's Word provides protection. It snaps my heart back to attention and helps me to run to him for rescue rather than try to fix things on my own. Psalm 31 demonstrates that King David knew this truth.

2. Know Where to Go to Get Your Happy

We have all kinds of wrong ideas about happiness. We think happiness is found in financial success. Yep. A big and beautiful house that looks like it would be featured on HGTV. A fancy new car. Designer handbags swinging from our shoulders. A nice shiny rock on our finger from our man. Stuff. That's it! Stuff will make us happy.

Or how about status? Having a fabulous job. One that is viewed as important or powerful. Maybe that is the key? To hold a position that is thought of as significant. Maybe status is our one-way ticket to the land of bliss.

However, neither stuff nor status holds the key to our happiness. The key is in our stance before God. David states, "I will be glad and rejoice in your unfailing love, for you have seen my troubles, and you care about the anguish of my soul" (Psalm 31:7 NLT). David realized that his joy could only come from his relationship with God, from knowing that he was utterly and fully loved. Loved with a love that would never fail. Never. *Ever*. Even when his enemies were pressing hard on every side tossing out accusations and hurling hateful words, David could still strike a vein of joy when he fixed his focus on God.

3. Realize the World Is Watching — and Learning

After declaring how great God's goodness is and how he has stored up blessings for those who honor him, David continues, "You have done so much for those who come to you for protection, blessing them before the watching world" (Psalm 31:19, my paraphrase). Yes, the world is watching how we respond. Are we going to retaliate when others are talking about us? Are we going to put our hope in our own damage control? Or will we allow those who are watching to see us stand still and put our trust in God. God rescues us and provides protection. And our willingness to trust God when we are on the receiving end of gossip can help a watching world to trust God as well. As we do our part to fix our focus on God and place ourselves in his care, we affirm that his power and protection are real.

How to Stop Gossiping

Okay. So perhaps we've gotten some direction about how to respond when we are victims of gossip. But what can we do to make sure we are not the ones who are doing the gossiping?

I've tried all kinds of things to try to keep myself from talking about others when I shouldn't. Sometimes my methods worked. Other times I just kept yacking. And when gossiping with others, I mistakenly felt secure in thinking that the person I was talking to would not tell the little morsels to the person being gossiped about. Boy, was I wrong! In fact, I can say with almost absolute certainty that if a person is willing to listen to gossip they are also willing to spread it. Or to betray your confidence. Or even to turn traitor and gossip about you! An old Irish proverb claims, "He who gossips with you will gossip about you." It's true.

I decided to try something else. When I was newly married, a little "gossip grid" was going around. Posting this convicting checklist near your phone was supposed to keep your tongue tied when it wanted to wag. It goes like this: *When considering whether to chatter about something, ask yourself first: Is it kind? Is it true? Is it necessary?*

So I scratched that little three-part golden rule of gossip out on a note card and prominently posted it in our tiny one-bedroom apartment where I was sure to see it daily. It worked for a little while. But then my mind engaged in a pretzel-bending round of mental gymnastics. Somehow I could justify that what I was saying was true. And it was necessary that I told it to the person on the other end of the phone. And being truthful is certainly kind, right? The little note card soon came down because it didn't help me keep my big mouth shut.

It was then that I turned to the same place David turned, God's Word. From this how-to-live-life manual we can unearth treasures that will help us to break the grip of gossip. Here are three practices that have worked for me.

1. Study How the Bible Describes a Gossip

The Bible is full of phrases that describe a gossip and also the effects of their actions. Committing these verses to memory did much more to prevent me from gossiping than mental visualization or a three-part ditty. Here are some of my favorites, along with their less-than-flattering depictions of gossips.

A Gossip Betrays Confidences

A gossip betrays a confidence,
> but a trustworthy person keeps a secret.
(Proverbs 11:13)

Nobody likes a Benedict Arnold: a person who betrays someone. Betrayal paints a picture of going to an enemy with information that will wound your friend. But a trustworthy person is admired. By refusing to participate in gossip, I can be known as a loyal and trustworthy woman rather than a traitor.

People Avoid a Gossip

A gossip betrays a confidence
so avoid anyone who talks too much.
(Proverbs 20:19)

Wow! People will avoid me if I am known as a gossip. And I've actually experienced this. There were certain people who just never seemed to want to be my close friend. In retrospect, I'll bet it was because I gossiped, and all these people were good at holding their tongues. I should also take this verse as a warning. I need to watch who I hang around. If I am prone to hang around someone who gossips, I am more likely to engage in gossip myself.

A Gossip Stirs Up Conflict

A perverse person stirs up conflict,
and a gossip separates close friends. (Proverbs 16:28)

Let's face it. There are some people who just like to stir the pot. Some who thrive on drama. But these social shenanigans often cost us friendships. Do we want the pot stirring traced back to us? I'd rather be known for dishing up a hearty batch of my famous cheesy corn chowder than for stirring up a bunch of drama in my circle of friends. If relationships are damaged and feelings are wounded, do we want our words to be the cause? And just knowing that the Bible uses the word *perverse* to describe such a person should make us stop and think the next time we are tempted to participate in gossip.

A Gossip Is Wicked

They have become filled with every kind of
wickedness, evil, greed and depravity. They are full

of envy, murder, strife, deceit and malice. They are gossips. (Romans 1:29)

When I happened on this portion of Scripture one day, it smacked me upside the head. Paul describes all sorts of awful, sinful behavior. Big stuff like murder, greed, malice, depravity, wickedness. These are sins we tend to rank high up on the evil scale. But tucked neatly away in this staccato string of serious sins is *gossip*. Wait! Back up the train. You mean my sharing a little juicy bit of gossip is right up there on the evil scale with killing someone?

We tend to rank sins, but that is not God's way of thinking. Sin in the Bible is portrayed by using an old archer's term of "missing the mark." Anything other than dead center in the bull's-eye is sin. So yes, someone who commits murder misses the mark by a country mile, but someone who gossips also misses the mark even if by just a short city block. Therefore, both are sin. The consequences of those sins vary in degree, but both are still considered sin in God's eyes.

Whenever we sin, repentance is required. Repentance is simply agreeing with God about our wrong and then doing an about-face and walking in the other direction, committing the sin no more. We won't be perfect. There will still be times that we give in to our sinful desires and choose the wrong path. However, the more we grow in our faith, the less frequent our sinning streaks should be.

My personal Bible study on gossips has helped me to keep my lips zipped more often. I didn't want to be viewed as a turn-coat or have others avoid me. And, although I loved being a pot stirrer through young adulthood, I soon discovered the more I stirred the pot the more likely the boiling hot liquid was to splatter and burn me too. But what helped me most was realizing that the Bible lumps gossip together with murder (Romans 1:29).

Murder slays the body. Gossip scorches the heart.

You've heard the old saying "Sticks and stones may break my bones but words can never hurt me"? Well, I beg to differ.

My oldest son had a jagged rock chucked at him once. It dinged him right in the old noggin causing a big goose egg that lasted about a week. An incoming stick once hit my other son during a rowdy play session in our friends' wooded lot. That wound eventually healed over too. I think a more accurate take on the catchy sticks-and-stones chant would be this: "Bruises fade and bones heal, but a scorched heart may take years to mend."

My words of gossip have scorched other's hearts. I know they have. At times, what I've said about others has gotten back to them, and they were crushed. I am someone who hates physical violence; I can't even stand to see it portrayed on screens. I'd never dream of hurling a rock or stick, and I'd certainly never dream of committing murder!

But I *have* wounded and killed with my words.

Knowing God included gossip on an index that also includes murder has caused me to take it more seriously. I regularly ask God to reveal to me if I owe someone an apology. It is a painful prayer, because he is always faithful to answer. And yes, I've had to go to a few people over the years and ask for their forgiveness. It's humbling — and it's healing.

I challenge you to pray the same prayer. Be warned — you might need to develop a taste for your own words since God may require you to go back and eat them. But trust me, once you do, there is no bitter aftertaste. Only blessed relief.

2. Keep Quiet

In addition to memorizing verses about gossip, there is another option that can help us avoid getting tangled and tripped by our own words about others. It is the choice to simply keep quiet.

Scripture states that there is a time to speak up and a time to remain silent (Ecclesiastes 3:7). Cultivating the habit of keeping quiet when others are gossiping is a little awkward and even painful. However, I have seen its fruit in my own life. I am much less likely to regret my words if I don't start even one sentence down the road that might lead to gossip, not taking the bait when another person throws out an enticing line or two trying to reel me in and get me to gossip. And I have noticed that others tend not to gossip as much around me if they know they may be met with silence in response.

I remember the first time I was in a group of girls when this happened. It was my freshman year of college, and we were all sitting around my tiny, cinder-block dorm room when the topic of someone on campus came up. One by one, everyone chimed in, giving their two cents' worth about this person. That is, everyone but my roommate. She sat silently on the bed with her legs crossed, staring out the window. Even when directly asked, "Don't you think so too?" she said nothing. Finally, one of the girls asked her if she was listening. Her reply was classic. "Oh, yes. I am listening all right. And I don't think I have anything to say. We shouldn't be talking like this behind her back."

The silence that followed was deafening. But I learned a good lesson that day. My roommate was right. None of us would have wanted others to talk about us, so why were we so eager to jump in and do the talking? Yes, perhaps the most effective way to avoid gossip is to simply keep our lips zipped. And if you want another powerful tool to keep your lips zipped, you might want to try what I started doing a few years back.

3. Make a Promise — Keep a Commitment

Years ago, I received a call from someone wanting to know if I had read the big city newspaper that day. I hadn't. But I really didn't need to because the voice on the other end of the line soon started relating all the details about a news story that took place in the small town where I lived at the time. The caller asked if I knew a person whose name was mentioned in the article. This person had been arrested for a crime, and the offense would likely result in a long prison sentence.

I did know this person. A close relative of theirs was one of my friends. My heart ached as I thought about what my friend might be going through since she was totally blindsided by the whole situation. Soon my phone started to ring and I began hearing the "ding" of the computer alerting me that I had new email messages.

I knew it was wrong to talk about this situation with other people, so I did not pick up the phone, and I ignored the emails because I was afraid someone might mention the incident to me. I wanted so much to honor God — and my friend — and to not gossip about this situation. It was then that I felt God nudge me, saying, "Really? Then tell *her* that."

So I grabbed my cell phone and sent my friend a text message. I told her she was loved and treasured, that I could not imagine what she was going through, and then I texted this: *I just want you to know that I will not be talking about this situation to anyone other than God. Please let me know how I can pray for you. And if you want to talk or need anything at all, call or text me. We love you.*

I wanted the Lord to help me refrain from idle talk about what was going on in this family. The psalmist writes, "Set a guard over my mouth, LORD; keep watch over the door of my lips" (Psalm 141:3). By contacting my friend and making a direct commitment to her, I felt like I was — in a tangible way — setting a "guard over my mouth." And if I ever did feel tempted to bring up the situation, I zipped my lips before I could let any words emerge. I simply did not want to go back on a promise to a friend or to God.*

Making this commitment to my friend was life-changing for me. Because I promised her I would not gossip, I didn't. (Go figure!) If someone else brought up the situation, I simply let them know that I had made a commitment to my friend that I wouldn't discuss the situation with anyone other than her and God. The promise helped me to refrain from gossiping, and it also encouraged a few other people to do the same thing in their lives.

Okay. I'm sorry if this section has sent any of you to Google to locate the number of the nearest podiatrist since I've now stepped all over your toes. Be assured my own pedicured piggies have been stomped on numerous times too by the Bible's advice on gossip. But friends, we can't go wrong when we choose to obey Scripture. Even the toe-crushing, oh-so-hard-to-do parts.

Did any of the verses you read above prick your conscience as you read them? Could God be asking you to make a call, send a text, or craft a private message to someone to ask forgiveness? Will you commit to not discussing what is happening in someone's life that others might find newsworthy in a gossipy sort of way? If so, do it soon. You won't be sorry.

Caught on Tape

There have been incidents in the news recently of public figures being caught on tape saying awful things. For some, these secret tapings have cost them not only their job or their political campaign but their reputation as well. And, of course, they've caused an outrage on Twitter. A firestorm on the Internet. I would haz-

---

* I have my friend's permission to tell this story.

ard a guess that if these people had known their remarks were going to be broadcast to the world, they certainly wouldn't have said them.

Why does knowing our words might leak out to others cause us to reevaluate what we say in the first place? Because of the consequences. We don't want our image tarnished. We don't want to lose face — or our livelihood. So perhaps we would do well to note that every word we utter is heard by our heavenly Father. What is whispered in secret is known to him. Why, the Bible says he knows our thoughts before they are even formed into words! Perhaps my mama was right. We need to care more what God thinks than about what others do.

How about we try to tie our tongues a little more frequently in the future? Knowing how devastating repeating hearsay and speaking words of gossip can be should keep us from participating in this verbal form of destruction. Instead of a little three-point checklist, how about we tape this up next to our kitchen sink instead:

I can *hear* you.
Love, God

8

LYING, LOVING, AND PEOPLE PLEASING

On Flattery and Speaking the Truth in Love

In trying to please all, he had pleased none.

AESOP

I was struck early with what has been called the "disease to please." While there might be a variety of reasons men and women come down with this sickness, still the symptoms are eerily similar.

The disease to please causes you to tell your mother-in-law how wonderful her lima bean casserole is when in reality all you want to do is spit into your napkin when no one is looking.

The disease to please makes you tell your best friend that the new, pastel, ruffled skirt she is wearing makes her look oh-so-slim when the truth is it makes her look like a puffy, pink lamp shade better suited to a baby nursery.

The disease to please beckons you to assure your husband he still is strikingly handsome and youthful looking even though most of his hair is gone. (Well, maybe that is attributed more to your love for him than to this disease.)

This serious illness makes you say all kinds of untruths with a smile on your face just to make someone else feel good or to get their approval or win them over as a friend. But even though others may walk away from the conversation feeling good, sometimes we ourselves feel bad. In fact, we are sure that we have just lied. But is this lying justified?

There is a tension we have to manage in situations like this. It's the tension between saying what is 100 percent true and being kind or considerate. People pleasing ramps up this tension. You want to be liked and accepted. However, you also know you should speak the truth. When you fear the truth may sting a little, you are tempted to tweak that truth ever so slightly (or more than slightly). Now what you are left with is a half-truth at best. But as we teach our children, a half-truth is still a whole lie.

People pleasing has landed me in a heap of trouble on several occasions. Whether it was wanting to please the popular crowd in school or hoping to find favor with the pastor's wife at the church where my husband just came on staff, I often whipped out my verbal charcoal pencil and shaded the truth just enough to morph it into something I knew someone else wanted to hear. Take, for instance, the case of the klutzy cheerleader . . .

To Cheer or Not to Cheer — That Is the Question

Throughout my adult life I have been involved in either coaching or judging both cheerleading and dance squads. The competitions are fun to watch, and just being around them makes me feel young. Each time I come away from an event, I'm just sure I can still do a round-off back handspring. (But I know better than to try. I don't want to end up in the local ER as the crazy middle-aged woman who thought she still had it but found out it was looooooong gone.)

Once during my coaching days, a friend decided that her daughter would make a fabulous cheerleader. Her girl had always dreamed of donning one of the red and white uniforms worn by the team of chanting girls, so this mama encouraged her to try out that spring.

At practice, the girls worked on the cheers and stunts required for tryouts. As I made my way around the school cafeteria checking on the various groups who were practicing their routines, I came upon the group that my friend's daughter was in. I had them line up for their cheer and perform it for me.

This particular cheer contained lots of jumps and kicks and intricate movements with the hands and feet, because having a cheer that encompassed all of the required components was the easiest way to select the best ten girls for the squad. As I watched my friend's daughter attempt to keep up with the rest of the group, my heart sank. Not only did she lack rhythm and skill, her facial expressions betrayed her exertion as she tried desperately to complete all the maneuvers. It was a cartwheel and pom-pom train wreck.

A few days later I ran into my friend. She asked how her daughter was doing at the practices. She told me what a fabulous time her daughter was having and how her hopes were set so high on being chosen as one of the ten girls to make the squad. I wanted to be honest with my friend, really I did. But I also wanted her to like me and not be offended by how I might answer. Every fiber of my being wanted to speak the truth, which in its raw form was something like this: "I'm sorry to disappoint you, but your daughter does not have what it takes to make the squad. She tries her very best but simply can't keep up. In fact, of all the girls trying out she is probably the worst, and there is no way she will be chosen once the judges' panel gets a look at her."

That is what I wanted to say, but I knew it was too harsh. And I feared it might make her want to ditch me as a friend if I said it.

Instead, I aligned my thoughts for a moment and then spit out something vaguely complimentary along these lines: "Wow! Your daughter sure is a hard worker when she wants something really bad. She is doing a great job trying to learn all of the routines to be ready for tryouts."

Because I didn't say she was skilled, my friend probed further.

"Well ... Do you think she's going to make it?"

Oh no! I was being asked such a straightforward question to which the only answers were the words *yes* or *no*. I did some quick thinking and then finally blurted out, "Well, you know. Since I am the coach of the team I really shouldn't be commenting on that. What if it got around to the other parents? Besides, I don't select the squad. I have a panel of four judges come in from out of the district to keep everything fair. Just tell her to keep working hard. I'm sure everything will turn out just fine."

Ugh! While I was trying frantically to navigate this verbal slippery slope, my friend was trying to read between the lines. Apparently, the conclusion she came to was this: I thought her daughter was fabulous but just didn't want to say it out loud to her for fear of it leaking out. Her daughter continued to show up to tryouts each and every day for two weeks. And she didn't improve one single bit.

When the day of tryouts came, the girls, all in their beribboned ponytails and sparkling clean sneakers, filed into the gymnasium. They performed in groups and also alone. When it came time for my friend's daughter to appear in a group in front of the judges, it was quickly apparent she just could not cut it. Her motions were behind the timing of the other girls, and when they performed a jump or stunt, she nearly fell over. Her solo appearance was even worse. She tried so very hard — bless her heart — and the expressions on her face showed it. Instead of looking like she was leading a crowd of cheering fans, she looked like she was trying to pass a kidney stone!

Some of the other girls began to giggle. I shot them a look to try to get them to stop, but it only made things worse. You know how it is when something seems so funny that you just simply cannot contain your laughter? Then the giggles become contagious and jump from person to person till you have a snickering mob on your hands. This was one of those times. Luckily, my friend's daughter was nearly done, and so she finished her individual cheer and then went and sat on the sidelines, where the laughing had fortunately died down.

When tryouts were finished and the scores were tallied, this brave girl was not one of the names called off for the new cheerleading squad. She burst into tears and quickly gathered her backpack and jacket and went out into the parking lot to wait for her mom to pick her up. My heart sank as I saw her standing on the curb, shoulders heaving up and down with uncontrollable sobs. I wanted to go out and put my arm around her, but I didn't. Instead I sat inside the now empty gymnasium mentally beating myself up. *Ugh! Why didn't you tell her mom the truth even if it meant she wouldn't like you anymore? Maybe if you had been straightforward with her, this would have never happened.*

A few days later, I talked with her mom. She said her daughter had had a rough night after the tryouts but since then seemed to have perked up a bit. I tried to console her because I could tell her mama heart was hurt to see her baby be so disappointed. I sat silently praying that she would not ask me my opinion about her daughter's cheerleading skills. But she did. She wondered if I thought the judges had made the right decision by cutting her from the squad. As painful as it was, this time I told her the truth, agreeing with the judges and softening the verdict with a lot of words about so many talented girls coming out for the squad this year. We finished our conversation and each went on our way. However, that whole incident caused me to rethink what I say and how and why I say it.

If only I had been brave enough to gently tell her my opinion of her daughter's cheerleading skills, perhaps she would have discussed with her daughter the likelihood of making the cut and whether trying out was a risk she wanted to take. Perhaps then the girl would've pursued a different interest, one that she was proficient at. I won't ever know for sure, but I can't help but wonder if speaking the truth in love that day might have saved this sweet young thing embarrassment and emotional devastation.

My people-pleasing ways caused quite a mess back then. It also caused me to shade the truth in an effort to keep a friend. Even though it is still so hard for me to do, I attempt to tell the truth gently. I try not to allow the fear of being straightforward (and thus possibly making someone "unfriend" me in real life) make me tell a twisted half-truth or — worse yet — an all-out lie.

Face-to-Face Flattery

Why do we do the people-pleasing dance? Why is it so hard to tell the truth when we think a lie is what the other person wants to hear? Do we do it to keep friendships? To prevent hurt feelings? So that we will still be liked by the other person?

Yes. Yes. And yes.

But it isn't just when we are asked questions that we are tempted to tell a slight variation of the truth. Sometimes we come up with pleasant lies all on our own without ever being asked. This is a different type of speech. It is called flattery.

Along with my other misguided gifts of gab, I am very skilled at wielding the clever tool of flattery. It has been said that gossip is saying something behind someone's back that you would never dare say to their face. However, flattery is the opposite. It is saying something to someone's face that you would never say behind their back — usually because you don't really believe it is true.

Flattery is perhaps the purest form of people pleasing. People pleasing becomes an ingrained habit when we need the approval of others in order to feel good about ourselves — to feel acceptance, love, and approval. And who doesn't approve of someone who says nothing but complimentary things about them? Flattery, like other weaknesses, sometimes starts out as a strength.

Throughout my life, I have been known as an encourager. Several members of our speaking-in-ministry team at Proverbs 31 call me the team cheerleader. I love to speak words that build others up. I love to encourage people to try things that they think might be too difficult for them. I love to write notes and send texts and post words on Facebook walls that make others smile and help them believe in themselves. But just as the strength of being decisive can morph into the weakness of being bossy, and the strength of being thorough can become the weakness of procrastination, the strength of encouragement can become the weakness of flattery. And my encouragement/flattery skills were honed early on.

If I wanted to be friends with a pretty and popular girl at school, I learned to say flattering things to her. I told her that her new poncho was simply adorable and totally brought out the color of her light blue eyes when in reality it reminded me of my grandmother's curtains! I knew this little lie of flattery might very well earn me a seat next to said popular girl at lunchtime later that day. Or perhaps she would choose to play double Dutch with me at recess, something she'd never done before. And what was the harm? My little lie gained me access to a coveted spot in the elementary school social circle.

School wasn't the only place that I learned to speak with flattering lips. I also knew it could get me places at church or within my family. Or on the drama team. Or with the neighborhood kids. The more people I told just what they wanted to hear, the more friends I gained (or so I thought).

At first, the habit of flattering others seemed pretty innocent. It really didn't get me into a great deal of trouble. I would give someone a compliment that I really didn't believe to be true. The other person happily accepted the compliment. No harm. No foul. But when I was asked a question that required me to choose between two different people, then I would find myself caught in a tangled web of my own words.

When I was just a freshman in college, I auditioned for the school musical and got a part in the chorus. There were several upperclassmen girls who were trying out for the leading role, and I really wanted to impress these girls and get to be in their circle of friends. So I reached into my verbal arsenal and grabbed my tool of flattery. There was one particular senior, we'll call her girl A, who was considered popular and pretty and a shining role model at our Christian college. I really wanted to be her friend.

Then there was a girl who was a junior (we'll call her girl B) who was also very well liked and talented. On separate occasions, I told each girl that I thought she deserved the leading role in the play. *She* had the best acting skills. *She* had the best vocal ability when it came to singing the show tunes. I assured each one that hands down, *she* would land the role of the leading lady.

I'm sure you already know where this is going. Yep. One day

I was gone from rehearsal. Girl A and girl B were paired together to work on a particular piece of music. As they were interacting and trying to learn the score, the subject came up of who would get the leading female part. The first gal said she was pretty nervous about trying out but had gained confidence because someone had told her they thought she would get the leading lady role hands down. The second girl, trying to be humble, gently corrected the first girl, saying that she was also told by someone that she was the very best actress and singer in the whole troupe. When each of them wanted to know who it was that said these things, of course they came up with the same name. And then? My name was mud. Neither of those girls ended up being my friend. My flattering words backfired.

When you speak flattering words, you paint yourself into a corner — a very lonely corner. In short order, you can go from being liked to being known as a people-pleasing liar. Flattery may seem like it wins you friends, but in reality it will likely cost you friends in the end.

Hapless Herod

Once upon a time in the days when Jesus walked the earth, there was a mighty king. His name was Herod Antipas. He had a wife who wanted him to do her a favor. Her name was Herodias. The Mrs. didn't really care too much for the man known as John the Baptist — the wandering prophet who ate wild locusts and honey and talked about repenting for the kingdom of God was coming soon. In fact, she'd just as soon have him dead.

John was a truth teller. On numerous occasions when he bumped into old King H., he brought up the little matter of the king and his bride. John pointed out the fact that it hadn't been right for Herod to marry her. In fact, it was downright illegal.

His wife was the former spouse of Herod's brother Philip. Apparently, it was against the law for him to marry her. But hey, he was the king. I guess he could do whatever he wished.

Herod arrested John and would have had him put to death, but he was afraid it might cause a riot because all of the people believed John was a prophet. And so, because of what all of the people thought, Herod chose to let him live. His actions were swayed because of the desire of the crowd.

Then one day Herod hosted a party to celebrate his birthday. For entertainment at the gala, his wife's daughter performed a dance that Herod — and all the guest judges on *Dancing in the Palace* — gave perfect tens. And so, right there in front of all of the party guests with their pointy hats and honking party blowers, the king made an oath to the belly dancer. He promised to give the young woman anything she wanted.

Apparently, she didn't have anything on her wish list that day because she initially gave no answer. However, she talked to her mother about it, and her mom had an idea. She urged her daughter to make this her request: "Give me here on a platter the head of John the Baptist" (Matthew 14:8).

Herod was greatly distressed at this request. This was not something he wanted to do, but he went ahead and did it. Why? "The king was distressed, but because of his oaths and his dinner guests, he ordered that her request be granted and had John beheaded in the prison. His head was brought in on a platter and given to the girl, who carried it to her mother" (Matthew 14:9–11).

Because of his oaths and his dinner guests.

Initially, it was because of his wife that King Herod tossed John into jail. Then he kept John alive because he knew it would please the crowds. In the end, he shot off his mouth and had to kill John in order to save face and please his dinner guests.

These decisions — the arrest, not having John executed,

and then later serving up his head on the royal china — were all motivated by people pleasing. We don't really know what Herod thought of the whole issue. He couldn't seem to make up his mind. (In verse five it seems he wanted him dead. By verse nine he is sorry that John was to be killed.) We are given only a glimpse into why he took the actions he did. It was always to appease someone else.

Fighting the Disease to Please

The tragedy of the death of John the Baptist can teach us some important lessons in the fight against the disease to please.

1. Beware of Making Promises in Order to Impress Someone

So, do you recognize anything about yourself in Herod's story? I certainly do. Although it seems safe to say that people pleasing has never brought most of us to the point of having someone executed, we can still fall into a trap like Herod did. Especially when we shoot off our mouths just to impress, please, or appease someone.

When my youngest son was in middle school, he told me that "all" his friends were going south to a warm climate for spring break. We weren't planning any southbound excursion, so he was bummed. He didn't understand why we too weren't packing the car and heading for Florida. It was his first year at a new school, and I think he felt left out when the guys talked about their upcoming trips. He did discover the next day, however, that two newer friends were also staying at home.

Now, there is a fabulous and popular indoor water park just across the Ohio border, so my son came up with a brainstorm. I would take him there, and his two friends would come. When he asked if this was okay, I said, "I would love to take you, honey, but it just won't work. We don't know the families of those friends yet. They won't want me to take their boys to another state. Besides, I have writing to do, and it requires me to be online. I need to be home. If all this weren't so, I'd be happy to take you to that awesome place. But I'm sorry buddy. Looks like it won't work out."

Okay, half-truths again. Nothing in that narrative was a lie, but the real (and whole) truth is that the place was outrageously expensive, and we simply couldn't afford to go there even for one night — not to mention the high price of gas for the nine-hour round-trip. I wanted to tell my boy this reason, but I already knew he felt many of the other kids he hung out with were wealthier than us. I didn't want our son to think we couldn't afford nice trips. So to keep up a good image and rank right up there with the other moms now packing their sunscreen, I left this reason out.

Well, he mentioned the water park idea to his friends. Not an invite. Just a mention. Their parents said if we decided to go they were fine with their kiddos tagging along. We had plenty of mutual friends who would vouch for our parenting prowess. My son hopped online. Ta-da! Wireless Internet at the park. (This was a new feature back then, so I assumed it wasn't offered.) I could work while the boys slid down the torpedo slide. When I saw the excitement in his eyes after the discovery of these facts, I just couldn't say no. My husband — though not happy with the way I'd shot off my mouth — covered for me and agreed I could take the boys to the park.

I smiled on the outside, but inside, my stomach sank. I didn't want my husband to have to work overtime to cover this trip. I refused to put it on a credit card. I didn't know how I'd pay for it. Thankfully, I found a coupon online and then — much to my surprise and delight — a payment arrived from a project I'd forgotten about that covered most of the trip. (Whew!)

I escaped that one by the skin of my teeth. (I still wonder

what I would have done if that check hadn't arrived.) But in retrospect, I should have shot straight with my son. Then, I could have used it as a life lesson about what is important — not money. I could have told him we could pray about it for a few days. Then, when the check arrived, I could have pointed him to God's provision and perfect timing.

I am now more careful to watch my words so I don't have to do something I promised but really didn't want to deliver. Commitments can be costly. Some cost us money. Herod's cost John his life. So beware of making a promise just to impress, please, or appease someone else.

2. Let Your Words Be Few

In biblical times, when written legal documents were few and far between, oaths were taken very seriously. Perhaps it was an oath to another person as part of a business transaction. Maybe it was an oath that had to do with behavior or personal commitments. Whatever the case, oaths were not taken lightly. Not only were they spoken in front of others, oaths were also spoken before God. Here's what the Old Testament wisdom writer has to say to potential oath makers: "Do not be quick with your mouth, do not be hasty in your heart to utter anything before God. God is in heaven and you are on earth, so let your words be few" (Ecclesiastes 5:2).

When it comes to speaking an oath or boldly stating something we want to do, we need to keep this verse in mind. I admire people who let their words be few. I wish I were more like them. The fewer words we speak, the less chance we have of succumbing to the trap of people pleasing with dazzling declarations we will later wish we could take back.

Letting our words be few helps us avoid the people-pleasing snare. So does another little trick we can pull out of our handbags when we are asked a question.

3. Do Not Answer Right Away

If someone asks you to take on a responsibility or asks your opinion about something you aren't certain of, simply do not answer right away. Kindly tell them that you need time to think about it. To pray about it. If it is a responsibility you are being asked to take on, you need time to discuss it with your spouse or family members. Don't be quick to give an answer before you have really thought it through. Putting some distance between the asking and the answering often helps us to make the best choice — one based on pleasing God rather than pleasing people. And during this time frame, we can learn to practice allowing our words to be few. Oh, how difficult this can be for those of us who seem to constantly run our mouths. Choosing silence over words seems foreign to us. But it is an art we must cultivate. And it can save us a lot of heartache from poor decisions and failed promises.

4. Keep God at the Center of Your Plans

It is easy to say what you have planned to do in the near or distant future. It is natural to want to set goals, to have ambitions and desires for your career or your family. It isn't wrong to want to aspire to grow a business or grow a family or to tackle some other endeavor in the future. But while we might be excited about what tomorrow holds, we should stop short of boasting about what we are going to do.

The author of James puts it this way:

> Now listen, you who say, "Today or tomorrow we will go to this or that city, spend a year there, carry on business and make money." Why, you do not even know what will happen tomorrow. What is your life? You are a mist that appears for a little while and then vanishes. Instead, you ought to say, "If it is the Lord's will, we will live

and do this or that." As it is, you boast in your arrogant schemes. All such boasting is evil. (James 4:13–16)

It isn't wrong to give voice to our dreams. What we are cautioned against is boasting about tomorrow without God anywhere in the picture. We need to keep God's wishes at the center of our desires. We can strategize and plan, but we need to run our plans through the grid of God's plan. Having this mind-set is part of what sets us apart from the world. People in the world make plans according to what they feel is best for them, what will bring the most financial gain, or what will bring them notoriety and success. God invites us to make our plans according to what will be in line with his desire for us and what will bring glory to him, not ourselves.

In the same way, we need to make sure our words are first meant to please God, not our hearer. The apostle Paul offers a helpful perspective on this. We need to ask ourselves: "Am I now trying to win the approval of human beings, or of God? Or am I trying to please people? If I were still trying to please people, I would not be a servant of Christ" (Galatians 1:10).

So which will you be? A servant of the Joneses (all the people you want to impress and please) or a servant of Christ? I know which one I'd choose! In a heartbeat.

5. Know When to Eat Your Words and Admit Your Fault

Consider this little wisdom scenario from Proverbs:

My son, if you have put up security for your neighbor,
if you have shaken hands in pledge for a stranger,
you have been trapped by what you said,
ensnared by the words of your mouth.
So do this, my son, to free yourself,
since you have fallen into your neighbor's hands:

Go — to the point of exhaustion —
and give your neighbor no rest!
Allow no sleep to your eyes,
no slumber to your eyelids.
Free yourself, like a gazelle from the hand of the hunter,
like a bird from the snare of the fowler. (Proverbs 6:1–5)

Although this scenario refers to a financial transaction, I think it also applies to any words we "commit" to a hearer and then regret. When we get trapped by our words, we need to deal with the situation quickly, allowing no sleep to our eyes until we have gone and freed ourselves. I know that the times when my mouth has been a trap, I have been in anguish and emotional turmoil until I go back to the person and either clarify or apologize for what I've said.

I have a cosmetologist friend who runs a basement salon in a town about ten minutes from me. I love going to her to get my hair cut, not only because she does a great job, but because her overhead is so low she doesn't charge very high prices. But a few times getting my hair cut has gotten me into verbal trouble. Now please don't get an image in your mind of a gossipy beautician who wants to divulge all the town's secrets. My friend is a godly Christian who is one of the biggest prayer warriors I know. However, we do know a lot of the same people, and there are times when the subject of one or more of them comes up.

More than once I have started to say things I shouldn't and had to stop myself. There have been other times I didn't follow the little check in my spirit and continued talking to the point where I was now saying things that were just downright wrong. I was truly trapped by my words.

There were a few times I felt guilty as I drove back east to my little hometown. One time in particular I just couldn't get off my mind the fact that I had talked about another friend while I was getting my hair highlighted. What I said about her was true, but it certainly wasn't kind or necessary. I knew what I had to do. Before any more time passed, I picked up the phone and apologized to my hairdresser friend for what I had said. She was gracious and forgiving, but she did say she was a little surprised that I had talked like that since she knew I was friends with the person I was talking about. Because I apologized, I was more careful what I said next time we were together. And because I did it soon, the offense was over and the guilt was gone, and I didn't dwell on it.

In other situations, I have let days or weeks go by with a nagging guilt that I really needed to apologize. And — oh, how I hate to admit this — there have been a few instances where I let years go by before I did anything about it. In fact, just recently I sent a private Facebook message to someone from my college days that I had long ago offended with my words. Every time I saw her picture on Facebook, my conscience was pricked again. I knew I owed her an apology. I knew what I should do. But I kept putting it off because I was embarrassed to admit that after twenty-five years I still was haunted by what I'd said. The moment I hit "send" I felt freed like a bird from a steel cage. I knew that no matter her response, I had finally done the right thing. I was no longer tethered by a heavy chain of guilt for failing to admit my fault. (And apparently neither was she because she apologized for things she had said about me. Now, we can see each other's smiling profile pics without even a twinge of guilt.)

If you've ever flown in an airplane you may recall that when flight attendants review the plane's safety instructions, they mention what to do should there be an emergency landing and a need to quickly exit the aircraft. "Remember," the words coming from the loudspeaker will advise, "the closest exit may be behind you."

It is the same with words. If you harbor any guilt or regret about something you said in the past, either to or about someone else, you may wish to look for an escape plan to get out of the situation safely. It might mean contacting them by letter, phone, or privately online to offer an apology and ask for their pardon.

Remember, the closest exit may be behind you.

In order to avoid having to clarify or apologize to others as often in the future, let's learn to deliver our words according to a well-known phrase found in Scripture. It's about telling the truth. But even more, it's about how to tell it.

Speaking the Truth in Love

We've covered a lot of things *not* to say, so now is a good time to turn our attention to what we *should* say. Not people-pleasing words. Not flattery. Not boasting or presuming on the future. Just simple guidelines for the way God wants us to use our words.

If you've been a Christian for any length of time, chances are you're familiar with the apostle Paul's words about "speaking the truth in love" (Ephesians 4:15). What does this mean? I think it means two things: We need to tell the truth. But also, kindness matters.

When I am speaking truth to another person, I need to do so with gentleness and respect. If I have something that is hard to say and will be difficult for the other person to hear, I need to make sure I soften my words and reassure them of my love. I need to craft my words in such a way that they are helpful. When pointing out something that needs to be addressed, especially in the behavior of family members, I need to address the behavior without attacking the person. And I need to nestle my truth in a cushion of encouragement. I call this the Wunderbar Pretzel Sandwich approach.

My home state of Michigan is famous for a tourist town named Frankenmuth that provides a little taste of Germany right here in the States. My favorite restaurant there is the Bavarian Inn, where they serve German-inspired cuisine, including the Wunderbar Pretzel Sandwich. While I am not too fond of the meat inside, Kasseler Rippchen (smoked pork loin), the pretzel bun is to die for — chewy and moist on the inside with a crusty, slightly salty deliciousness on the outside.

We can deliver our hard truth words using the Wunderbar Pretzel Sandwich approach. The top half of the bun is an encouraging truth, so you start out with that. Then you speak your hard truth statement. That is the meat of the sandwich. And finally, you finish off with another encouraging truth, the second half of the bun. The person is more likely to listen to you if the hard truth is wrapped tightly in love and encouragement.

Let's rewind the tape and revisit my little encounter with the prospective cheerleader's mom. How could that scenario have gone down differently if I'd used the Wunderbar Pretzel Sandwich approach? I might have said something like this:

"I am so impressed with your daughter and her courage at trying something new. I can tell she is very determined because of the hard work and diligent effort I see her exerting in practice. However, because of the high caliber of talent and the number of girls with cheerleading experience trying out for the team this year, I am doubtful that your daughter, since she has no prior cheerleading experience, will make the squad. I would hate to see her feelings crushed, so I really need to be honest with you and let you know that I don't think she will make it. Perhaps it would be best if she channeled her determination into another sport or activity where she has more expertise and natural talent. With her hard work ethic, I'm sure she will excel at something that will bring her a lot of enjoyment. I'm just thinking cheerleading is not for her."

If I had spoken those words to my friend that day, it might have saved her daughter from the emotional and disappointing situation that followed. It would also have been the truth — honesty woven in charity. And even though I may have still feared I'd offend or lose my friend, I could have rested in the assurance that I tried my very best to be honest without being hurtful.

The Wunderbar Pretzel Sandwich approach. Maybe you could try whipping one up the next time you need to deliver difficult words in a delicate situation.

Finding the Fulcrum

Speaking the truth in love can be a hard balance to strike. Like tightrope walkers who must carefully find their center of gravity to avoid falling, we must find that tender place where we are both truthful and loving so our words don't offend or fall on deaf ears.

We shouldn't avoid telling the truth altogether, assuming it is unloving to do so. However, we also should not blurt out the truth critically and caustically with no concern for the other person's feelings. We must find the fulcrum — the pivot point that balances gentle honesty with hard truth enveloped in love. When we do this, we please the One who gave us the ability to speak in the first place. And we live out loud these truths expressed by the psalmist:

> LORD, who may dwell in your sacred tent?
>> Who may live on your holy mountain?
> The one whose walk is blameless,
>> who does what is righteous,
>> who speaks the truth from their heart;
> whose tongue utters no slander,

who does no wrong to a neighbor,
    and casts no slur on others;
who despises a vile person
    but honors those who fear the LORD;
who keeps an oath even when it hurts,
    and does not change their mind;
who lends money to the poor without interest;
    who does not accept a bribe against the innocent.
Whoever does these things
    will never be shaken. (Psalm 15)

May you speak the truth from a loving heart. May your tongue utter no slander. May you do no wrong to a neighbor and cast no slurs. May you weigh your words carefully and keep your oaths. And may you never be shaken.

9

HURLING HATE OR HEALING HEARTS

Containing Your Anger

"In your anger do not sin": Do not let the sun go down
while you are still angry, and do not give the devil a foothold.

EPHESIANS 4:26 – 27

I wrestled with several plastic grocery bags as my purse swung wildly from my shoulder. I was trying desperately to free up a hand to open the back door that leads from our garage into the kitchen. Tired from a long day of errands and appointments, I just wanted to get into the house, put the groceries away, and then collapse on the couch.

As I fumbled with my keys and stepped up onto the landing that leads into the kitchen, I nearly tripped and broke my neck. I also broke out into a horrible rant as I saw the reason for my near trip and fall.

"Kenna! Mitchell! Spencer! You kids get out here *right now* and take care of these shoes and boots. I am sick and tired of how you all just toss your shoes here with absolutely *no regard* for what I've told you. You know your shoes go on the rug. I don't want to *ever* see this junk lying here again. You hear me? You are all so lazy! Now I said get out here … *right now!*"

My kids heard me all right. So did half the neighborhood.

I have a major pet peeve about the shoes, sports cleats, boots, and flip-flops that collect in our garage. First, I'd prefer that each family member have only a pair or two there. (That day there were about nineteen, and only four were from my husband and me. The other fifteen or so were from our three darlings. Yes. Crunch the numbers. That's *five* pairs each!)

I also prefer that shoes be lined up neatly in a row on the lovely industrial rug that is strategically placed just to the right of the landing for my clan's convenience. I've even timed out how much longer it takes to actually place said pairs of shoes neatly on the rug instead of kicking them off haphazardly. Just three seconds!

But my kids couldn't seem to get with the program, and so? It made me angry. This wasn't the only time a domestic dispute broke out. There were other shouting bouts as well. Sometimes they were over issues of outright disobedience when I had specifically instructed a particular child to clean up a mess they had made. Other times it was over an accident: spilled grape juice on the light-colored carpet, too much laundry soap in the new front-loading washing machine, a screen door left open and now there were mosquitoes in the house. Many normal mishaps of childhood.

Although on the one hand it felt good to vent my anger, on the other hand it made me gulp in guilt for barking so angrily at my sweet children. Later, after the shoes were straightened and some even put away, I felt God tap me on the heart, prompting me to apologize to my kids. I fought it for a while, arguing that the kids were the ones who should be apologizing to me.

It was then that I felt God clearly say, "Mind your own sin, sweetheart."

Ouch. Yes, my kids' disregard of instructions wasn't right. Children should obey their parents (Ephesians 6:1). But when they don't? Well, I couldn't recall a single verse that then grants parents the right to holler and scream, giving all of the neighbors who were trying to eat their spaghetti supper both dinner *and* a show.

I apologized to my kids that night before they went to bed. I asked them to forgive me for my angry mama mouth. Then together we strategized about how we could remedy the whole footwear fiasco in the garage. I realized that part of the reason I was always badgering my clan to get with the program was that there was no good program for them to get with in the first place. The industrial rug just wasn't cutting it. So we cut the rug. With a trip to the department store and some nice wire shelves, we found a solution to the footwear conglomeration.

We compromised. I didn't get my entire desired neat-as-a-pin plan, but the modified version still worked better than the industrial rug. As a result, I no longer badger my poor kids about their shoes. My vocal cords aren't so sore, and the neighbors can now enjoy their dinner in peace.

Family Fume

One spring day, I sat in my backyard with my friend Suzy and our kids. While we relaxed in lawn chairs, sipping lemonade, a few of the children played on the swing set. The rest sat at our bright yellow children's picnic table, purchased just days earlier. They were happily creating masterpieces on the pages of several coloring books.

When it came time for lunch, I helped the children clear their coloring supplies off the table. As I gathered up the crayons and coloring books, I spied a frightful sight. One of Suzy's daughters had gone into the house and grabbed permanent markers to color with instead of the crayons. And color with them she did — all over the brand-new picnic table! She'd even written her name in her very best seven-year-old penmanship.

I was angry that our newly purchased picnic table was now laden with permanent red and purple graffiti. I wanted to raise my voice and shout and scream my displeasure. But I didn't. Instead, I leaned over and spoke gently to my friend's child.

"Oh, Kelly. Mrs. Ehman wants you to use crayons when you color, not markers. Would you please go put them back in the house? Thank you, honey."

My eldest child's jaw dropped when she witnessed my kind and calm reaction. Loud enough for everyone to hear, she said, "Man! It's a good thing it was you, Kelly, and not one of us. Mom would've hollered at us something awful if we'd done that!"

Ouch.

My daughter simply vocalized a truth she noticed in my life: I tend to lose my cool with my family, but somehow manage to keep calm when I interact with others.

The book of Proverbs describes a woman who is praised not only for what she *does*, but more importantly for who she *is* — specifically, how she interacts with people: "She opens her mouth with wisdom, and the teaching of kindness is on her tongue" (Proverbs 31:26 ESV). As a mom, there are many things I need to teach my children about the basic tasks and responsibilities of life. How to make their beds. How to unpack the groceries and put them away. How to do laundry without changing all of the white underwear to a rainbow-Skittle mix. And yes, I need to teach them how to keep their shoes from becoming life-threatening obstacles when they take them off in the garage. But when teaching them these things, do I do it with kindness, or is my tone caustic? Do I open my mouth with wisdom, or do

I just open my mouth, spewing out whatever is bubbling up in my angry heart?

I faced the music that summer day and owned up to the truth my child pointed out: I tend to extend grace to those outside my family — even complete strangers — while so easily snapping at the people within my home. Yes, there are times I must instruct and correct my kids. Yet when I do, I must be conscientious and kind while giving counsel. It's not always easy, but God is always available to help me not to be controlling, complaining, or critical.

Perhaps we would all do better to learn to pause before we pounce when interacting with our loved ones, treating them with the respect we tend to give others. Or better yet, to pause, pray, and then not pounce at all!

But how do we do that?

In Your Anger Do Not Sin

I have found that one key chunk of Scripture helps me to mentally work through the steps of anger and prevents me from doing and saying things I might later regret: " 'In your anger do not sin': Do not let the sun go down while you are still angry, and do not give the devil a foothold" (Ephesians 4:26–27).

I observe four helpful things in this passage when it comes to containing my anger.

1. We Are Going to Get Angry

Notice that it does not say, "Do not be angry. A woman who gets angry is sinning." Nope. Read it closely. It says, "In your anger do not sin." God created us with emotions, and anger is one of them. Feeling the emotion of anger is not the problem. The problem is when we let our anger trigger actions that result in wrongdoing.

2. Do Not Sin

Three simple little words, but they sometimes seem like an impossible feat: do not sin. What does anger taken into the level of sin look like? It might be shouting. Or sarcasm. Or belittling someone. It isn't verbalizing your displeasure over someone else's actions. If someone's actions have angered you, telling them in a straightforward and calm manner is a reasonable thing to do. Letting the anger escalate to the point of an outburst is what crosses the line into sin. Or if you're not the explosive type, there is equal opportunity for sin in letting angry feelings ice over into a wall of bitterness and resentment.

3. Deal with It — Pronto

Anger is inevitable. People are going to push your buttons — and you are going to push back. Or maybe their intent wasn't to tick you off, but you are hoppin' mad anyway. You hope to respond in a way that lines up with God's Word. But when you don't, and instead dwell on the offense, letting bitterness begin to boil up inside, you must address your anger — and fast! I know this from experience: the longer you stew, the more likely you are to strike. No wonder the Bible advises us to deal with anger promptly.

It's fine to pause, to step out of a tense situation and collect your thoughts, or in some cases to get counsel from a trusted advisor. But for most situations in life — and especially with family members — the wisdom of Scripture is to deal with it the same day. Dealing with it may mean stepping out of the meeting to make a phone call. It may mean waking up a sleeping child to ask for forgiveness. Do whatever it takes to verbalize your feelings in a rational manner and let your simmering emotions calm down — or let your icy demeanor thaw.

4. Be Aware of the Devil's Sneaky Wrestling Moves

Wrestling is one of the things my little midwestern town is well known for in our state. Our high school wrestling team has taken the state championship four years in a row. The head coach of the wrestling team just happens to go to my church, so I asked him about what it means to gain a foothold. I learned a lot in my mini grappler lesson.

The feet are very important in wrestling. The coach said that if you can wrap your foot around your opponent's foot causing him to lose his balance, you can wrestle him to the ground in an all-out pin. Then, once you get a foothold, you have a chance to get a stronghold, pressing his shoulder blades flat to the mat. And once you exert your strength over your opponent — if you are playing dirty — you can get him in a choke hold, knocking the life and breath right out of him. (Of course in wrestling this move is illegal!)

Wow. It's not hard to see the spiritual implications, right?

When Satan gets a foothold, we're in trouble. He wants us to lose our balance. He would love to pin us to the mat, rendering us ineffective for the kingdom. Once we give him a foothold, he can gain a stronghold over us and then go in for the choke hold, finishing us off. This passage of Scripture tells us just how Satan gets that first hold on us: when we fail to deal properly and promptly with our anger.

Using Ephesians 4:26–27 as a template for processing feelings of anger can prevent us from stewing and then striking, ultimately giving Satan the upper hand. Remember, possessing feelings of anger isn't wrong. What is wrong is when we allow them to fester and then we choose to fight. Weren't we taught long ago as children that fighting is neither healthy nor helpful?

I have found something I can do that is helpful in stopping

an argument or preventing one from ever starting in the first place. It not only has to do with my tongue. It is has to do with my tone.

Snuggly Words

I love my Snuggie®.

Yes, I am the proud owner of that "amazing blanket with sleeves." It was a surprise gift from my husband last year on Sweetest Day. He gave it to me that crisp October day, along with some dark chocolate, sort of as a joke. But do you know what?

I absolutely adore this wacky infomercial item!

Not only can I stay toasty warm in the Michigan winters whilst typing away on my laptop with my arms completely free and functional, but that cozy wrap is also the softest blanket I have ever owned. It just begs me to swaddle myself up inside its fluffiness and sit for a spell. My only trouble with it is that my kids often steal it for themselves!

Softness feels good. It calms me down. Comforts me. Makes me feel wanted and welcomed.

My words can be a Snuggie®. Yes, something soft and calming and comforting. Especially when it comes to answering a question posed to me by someone who is getting on my nerves. Let's consider the best (and softest!) way to respond when irksome questions come flying our way. For example:

"Mom? Where's my football jersey?"

"Honey, you don't mind if my mom comes to stay for a week, do you?"

"Mom? Will you make your oatmeal dried-cherry cookies for my first-hour class? There are thirty-two kids, and I told Mr. Billings you would make some for me to take. Oh yeah. Tomorrow." (Question posed at 10:15 p.m.)

"Do you mind sending me that information right away?" This from a coworker who has twice lost the emails in which I'd already sent her the information.

The biblical wisdom for responding in such situations is this: "A soft answer turns away wrath, but a harsh word stirs up anger" (Proverbs 15:1 ESV). Sadly, it's wisdom I don't always follow. I can snip. Be snarky. Escalate the combative climate by barking back with another question like, "Well, how am I supposed to know where your jersey is? I'm not the defensive tackle for the junior varsity football team, and it isn't my job to know where your things are, so deal with it, bubba. You can wear your sister's pink dance leotard for all I care!"

Ahem.

Un-soft answers only worsen the mama drama in my house. And they don't win many points with my coworkers or neighbors either. When we give an un-soft answer, we drizzle a little gasoline on the tiniest spark of a potential spat. It may combust and flare, setting off a big old blaze. However, when I am intentional about giving a gentle answer to (sometimes foolish) questions, it prevents the anger from escalating into an inferno. Don't be a gasoline queen, tossing even more propellant on an already heated conversation. Or, better yet, prevent that fire from ever igniting in the first place. (Smokey the Bear would be proud!)

Giving a soft answer doesn't mean I don't give a truthful one; I just give it in a respectful and kind manner. The mark of a soft answer is that it doesn't spark higher levels of friction and irritation but instead sets the stage for a healthy discussion. For example ...

"I don't know where your jersey is, but I need you to take charge of it yourself. I already have so many things I need to keep track of."

"What week are you thinking of? I'm snowed under right now, so even thinking about having a houseguest stresses me out."

"Honey, I wished you'd told me sooner about the cookies. I guess you're just going to have to disappoint your teacher. We can pick up some store-bought ones on the way to school."

"Here is that information. Lost emails are a bother, aren't they? I've had that problem too. You might try an archiving service."

On a scale of one to ten (with one being "never" and ten being "always"), what number would you say best describes how often you try to answer annoying questions in a soft and gentle way? (Don't feel bad. Before God greatly convicted me in this area, I'd have given myself a three!)

Will you commit with me to answering annoying questions in a soft and gentle way? To refuse to throw gasoline on a small spark that could ignite a fiery family feud or cause a ruckus with your coworkers? Will you work to defuse the fight before it even begins? Your family and friends might notice your effort and reward you by responding in kind. (Or maybe by even buying you your very own Snuggie®!)

Climate Change

Since anger is something most of us have to deal with on a regular basis, we must be armed and ready with a strategy for biting our bitter tongues. So let's get practical and do a little exercise that might help us to discover just when and why we become irked, so that we can work on some "climate change" in our very own home. Set aside some time to be alone and answer the following questions honestly. No one will see this but you.

- Briefly list the last three to five times you let loose of your anger verbally, unloading on your family.

- What commonalities do you notice in these situations? For example, people, circumstances, physical or emotional states, and so on.

- Based on what the events have in common, what patterns or triggers do you recognize about why or when your anger tends to get the better of you? Write down one or two for each event you listed.

- Which patterns or triggers happen most often? For example: *We are running late for school or church. I am interacting with a difficult coworker. I am tired.*

- Briefly consider any patterns that happen at home. What might you and your family members do differently to begin breaking the pattern? For example, do you have people at your house who need to pack lunches for school and work? Is there sometimes a squabble because all the granola bars have suddenly gone AWOL? We've started divvying up the trail mix, chips and other lunch items as soon as they're purchased labeling them by using a Sharpie marker or placing them in separate, marked plastic zip bags. That way, no one feels permission to eat a whole slew of granola bars for a midnight snack, leaving their parent or sibling without any for lunch the next day. It also prevents spats over such scenarios.

For one week I challenge you to make the most of your annoying question moments. How? Whenever that person who tends to bring out the mean in you asks one of those anger-inducing questions, silently count to three as you shoot up a prayer asking God to help you craft a truthful, helpful, and *soft* answer. See how gentleness changes the climate in your home and at work. God's Word is true: A soft answer helps to stop the stirring anger.

And if you feel the need for the occasional reminder, print out the Bible verse below and post it in a prominent place where you will see it often — the bathroom mirror, on a vehicle dash-board, or at the kitchen sink. Make it your goal to memorize this verse during the next week or so. When you are tempted to pounce, pause and recite the verse to yourself. And then? Don't let your anger make you sin. Lead you to instruct or speak truth? Yes. Explain? Sure. Correct and redirect? Yes, ma'am.

But not sin.

" 'In your anger do not sin': Do not let the sun go down while you are still angry, and do not give the devil a foothold" (Ephesians 4:26–27).

I Gotta Die

My fifteen-year-old son has a fondness for iPod games, especially ones where a creature has to jump, twist, dodge, and dart in an effort to stay alive. He often plays these games on our short commute to school each morning.

As we drive, we go over pick-up instructions for that particular day. At the middle school after wrestling practice? Or at the high school if there is optional weight lifting that day? And what time?

I also give my "Be sure your sins will find you out" lecture that my own sweet mama often gave me. The man-cub just keeps playing his game, acting as if he's not listening. But I know he is.

Sometimes when I'm jockeying for position in the parental car-pool line, I inform my boy it's time to get out of the vehicle. Still engaged in the game, he will say, "Hang on a second. I gotta die."

As in, "I'm still finishing this round. I don't want to power off just yet. Let my character finish this round until it dies. Then I will get out of the car."

As he said those words this morning, they spoke to my soul. As a follower of Christ, I am to die to self. But so often, I choose not to. Instead, I elevate self. I promote self. I think little of the other person and much of me. But before I react ... before I hurl a harsh word ... before I pass judgment or speak unkindly to my husband or snap at my child, perhaps I need to take a deep breath and say, "Hang on a second. I gotta die." Die to self. Die to flesh. Die to my "rights" that too often result in my wrongs. Yes, Paul said it best — "I die daily" (1 Corinthians 15:31 KJV).

Does this mean in everything?

Consider Jesus' statement, "Greater love has no one than this: to lay down one's life for one's friends" (John 15:13). My initial response is to imagine all the dramatic ways that could happen. I might jump in front of a car in order to get my friend out of harm's way. A soldier might willingly give up his life on the battlefield. A father might risk his life in a dangerous operation in order to donate an organ to his child.

But what if laying down one's life includes dying to self in the everyday details of life? In my interactions with others, especially those within my own family? These daily, hourly, and even moment-by-moment death decisions sometimes seem more difficult than the dramatic ones!

And if we're trying to die to self in our own strength, they will also be impossible. In order to die to self in the daily, routine hassles and relational challenges we face, we must draw deeply from the available power of the Holy Spirit, surrendering our life and words to his will.

So the next time you're tempted to react in a way that won't please God, remember my game-lovin' man-cub. Take a deep breath, a pause that centers your heart, snaps your soul to attention, and gently declare ...

"Hang on a second. I gotta die."

10 SOMETHING TO TALK ABOUT

Wonderful Ways to Use Your Words

A word fitly spoken and in due season
is like apples of gold in settings of silver.

PROVERBS 25:11 AMP

Words matter.

They can build up or tear down. They can impart wisdom or bring shame. They can deliver encouragement or deflate the spirit. Words can be a weapon or a healing balm. A welcome sound or a dreaded racket. And words can even change the world. Who knows just how many pivotal points in history would have been changed if someone had used their words differently.

What if, at the Virginia convention of 1775, instead of saying, "Give me liberty or give me death!", Patrick Henry had taken the podium and declared, "Ya know ... being under England's rule really isn't that bad. Sure the taxes are a little high on the tea and all, but fighting a revolution and forming a new country sounds quite exhausting, if ya ask me. Let's just keep things the way they are and we can all head down to the pub for a tall cold one. All right ... who's with me?"

What if, at his first presidential inaugural address in 1933, President Franklin Delano Roosevelt, speaking to the American people at the height of the Depression, had not said, "The only thing we have to fear is fear itself"? What if he had sheepishly mumbled instead, "I'm excited to be president. But I have to tell you that I am a little afraid of the future. Okay, *a lot* afraid! The economy is horrible. So many people don't have jobs. The political climate in the world is unstable, and I'm terrified there might be another world war. I think you should all stock up on food and lock all of your doors — and hurry! Something awful is headed this way."

What if President Ronald Reagan in West Berlin in 1987, instead of challenging the Soviet Union by boldly urging Mr. Gorbachev to "Tear down this wall!" had said, "Wow! That is a ginormous wall, Mikhail. I don't think I've ever seen one so big. But here's the thing, dude. Not to be mean or anything, but it's kind of ugly. Perhaps you should consider planting some nice climbing ivy along it. It might really spruce things up around here."

Yes, the course of history has been decided at times by courageous words spoken by courageous people. And their courageous words were contagious, igniting the same courage in others. That's actually the meaning of the word *encourage* — to impart courage to another. Just as important as knowing what not to say is knowing how to carefully craft our words to impart courage to others — and knowing the best time to say them.

I'm grateful for the courageous people of the past whose words and actions helped make the world a better place today. But I also thank God for the ordinary people in my personal past that imparted courage or showed kindness to me. Their words and ways helped to shape my life too. Recently, I took a quick trip back down memory lane to reflect on their impact on me.

Remembering

One wintery Saturday afternoon found me cleaning our basement storage room. There were boxes of papers to sort, bins
of holiday decorations to shuffle, and other assorted items that
needed to be neatly realigned on the shelves. I'd estimated it
would take me an hour or so to tidy up the space. Except I
hadn't factored in one thing.

Memories.

The items I straightened and stacked weren't spectacular;
they were the common articles found in many basements and
garages. But the fragrance of precious memories clung to them.
Memories of events that changed my life. Memories of people
who touched my heart. My cleaning pace slowed significantly.

I gently folded the ivory lace dress my daughter wore for her
baby dedication at church over two decades ago. My mother
bought it for her and continues to dote on her grandchildren,
picking up special gifts and treats for them. She has a knack for
making others feel loved.

I thank my God every time I remember my mom.

A hand-sewn stuffed bunny rabbit sat perched on a corner
shelf. My college roommate Kelly lovingly crafted it for my
daughter when she was young. For over thirty years, Kelly has
been a thoughtful friend who never forgets my birthday and who
faithfully prays for my family.

I thank my God every time I remember my friend Kelly.

I found an old key on a grayed leather key chain. Turning
the key chain over I saw a simple word scrawled across the back:
pool. Our former neighbor, a widow and retired schoolteacher,
had an in-ground swimming pool, and we did not. Without children or grandkids nearby, she gave us a key so our young family
could take a dip any time we wished.

I thank my God every time I remember Mrs. Beaufore.

Memories surrounded me as I sorted through yearbooks and photo albums. Old friends. Precious relatives. Former church members and coworkers. Pieces of my past. So many of these dear folks played a part in my life. Remembering them brought a smile to my face and a few tears to my eyes.

I whispered a prayer of sincere thankfulness for all of those people who helped shape my life. Their encouragement, advice, and sometimes mere presence were blessings to me. God even used the relationship bumps to help mold my character and teach me life lessons.

When addressing the church in Philippi, the apostle Paul wrote to the believers, declaring, "I thank my God every time I remember you" (Philippians 1:3). Just calling to mind the image of these loved ones gave the apostle reason to be grateful to God. But Paul didn't only thank God — Paul also told his friends of his gratitude.

He used his words.

And we can do the same. After thanking God for these precious people, we can use our words to thank them directly, verbally or in writing. It really doesn't take that much time to briefly step out of our daily routine and devote a moment or two to shooting off an email, making a phone call, or even sending a handwritten note to someone about whom we would say, "I thank my God every time I remember you." Expressing gratitude brings contentment, and contentment brings peace — peace in knowing God fits together all the pieces of our lives to make us who we are today.

So here is a challenge. Will you carve out some time today to use your words to encourage — to intentionally bless others? It really is very easy. Grab a pen or pick up your phone. Someone is waiting to hear how thankful you are for them. It might just make their day. And yours.

LOVE PROMPTS

Got a minute? Grab a pen! Use any of these prompts to get you started on jotting a note, an email, or a text to a loved one in your life. For some, the statement stands alone. For others, elaborate on the thought that is given. Your words are sure to bless your recipient!

Five Powerful Phrases to Speak to Your Spouse

I trust your judgment.
I'm glad I married you.
Here is what I appreciate most about you …
I am with you.
Being your wife has taught me …

Five Powerful Phrases to Speak to Your Child

You can do it.
A happy memory I have of when you were younger is …
I am confident you can make good choices.
Being your mom has taught me …
God has an amazing life planned for you.

Five Powerful Phrases to Speak to Your Parent

I'm not sure if I've ever told you before, but thank you for …
A wonderful memory I have of my childhood is …
I admire your strength.
How can I help you?
I am proud of you for …

Five Powerful Phrases to Speak to Your Friend

My favorite thing about our friendship is …
The best time I ever had with you was when …
I am with you all the way.
The character quality I most admire in you is …
You remind me of Jesus when you …

Lenten Letters

For the last two years during the Lenten season leading up to Easter, I have tried a new spiritual practice. While I did not grow up in a church that observed Lent by giving something up for forty days, the practice always intrigued me, and so I did it anyway. One year it was chocolate. One year it was soda. And one year I tried making it meat. But I loved me a good quarter pounder with cheese, so that pledge didn't last very long!

For the last two years, I have observed the forty days of Lent in a different way. I decided that rather than give up something, I would take on something. And so I trekked off to the local department store and purchased forty cute note cards (on the clearance rack — whoo-hoo!). Then I stopped by the post office and purchased forty cute stamps. (I mean, I love and respect the American flag and all, but nothing cute-i-fies a letter quite like an adorable, whimsical stamp.) I placed the note cards and stamps, along with my address book, in a rustic wicker basket and nestled it between the two chairs in our living room. Then, each morning upon rising, or each evening before bed, I took about three minutes to write an encouraging note to someone in my life.

One day I wrote to an old friend whom I hadn't seen in ages. I recalled happy memories and explained to her just how thankful I was that our paths had crossed all those years ago. The next day I felt prompted to jot a few lines to the teenager who had sung in the worship team at church that weekend. I knew she had been very nervous trying out for the team and even more afraid of her first appearance on the platform at church. I declared what a bang-up job she did and how proud I was of her. Still another time I decided to send a message to our neighbors down the street, letting them know how much our family enjoyed their elaborate and Christ-centered Christmas decorations each year. Their entire house, as well as a long line of pine trees at the edge of their property, made a beautiful display, especially when the snow was falling. We enjoyed its breathtaking and nostalgic appearance every year, but I had never told them just how much we did.

My little note-writing marathon was a wonderful experience. So many of the people to whom I sent a letter contacted me to say just how much it meant to them. All day long we see words and are inundated with language. Most often this comes in the form of electronic words. We read tweets. We scroll through Facebook statuses. We read memos and answer emails. We work our way through our favorite blogs. But very seldom do we get an old-fashioned, handwritten sentiment delivered to our mailbox.

Writing these notes brought out something good in me: gratitude. As I acknowledged my gratitude to each person, I began to take on an attitude of thankfulness. So often I am not the most grateful person. While I am an outgoing gal who is often thought of as the life of the party, I can also view the world through very critical eyes. When I look at life through the lens of criticism, the delight can drain right out of my day. I begin to dwell on what's wrong with my life. What isn't right about the grocery store setup. What I wish the bank tellers would do differently. But when I stopped and disciplined myself to pen my gratitude on a piece of paper each day, it shifted my perspective.

Instead of rolling my eyes at the grocery store bagger who was moving as slow as molasses on a day I was in a rush, I thanked him for bagging my goodies faithfully for the last ten years. He is a mentally challenged man, and when I spoke these words to him his entire face lit up. Rather than sit in my idling car stewing because the coffee drive-through line was taking so long that morning, I greeted the drive-through worker with a smile and words of appreciation. And then I handed her a gift card to the local bakery to grab a sweet treat for her break that day. When I saw a clumsy teenager trying to wrestle a dozen shopping carts in a parking lot during a snowstorm, I rolled down my car window and handed him a $20 bill. I told him that grocery cart–getters should get tips too, and his hard-work ethic each week when I saw him there had really impressed me.

Do you notice what happened here? My thoughts of gratitude led to words of thankfulness. And along with those words came a call to action. I not only wanted to *say* something kind to these people, I wanted to *do* something kind for them as well.

So just who in your life might be waiting to receive helpful, healing, and hopeful words from you? Family members — even the ones with whom you may have a less than lovely relationship? Coworkers, the people with whom you share an office space? Neighbors? Church members? The necessary people in your life? Necessary people are the ones who help us do life. The postal worker. The doctor or dentist. The person who does our nails or cuts our hair. Why, even the garbage collector! Each day you encounter many people, either face-to-face or perhaps online. If you aspire to be an "on-purpose person" who reaches out and speaks life to at least one person each day, I guarantee your words will not only cheer them, they will change you.

As I've already said, words matter. They have tremendous power to affect us either for the positive or the negative. Most of us can recall words spoken to us that have either spurred us on or completely devastated us. I can vividly recall two such incidents in my own life.

Words that Hurt — Words that Heal

The first incident happened when I was in high school. I was raised in a single-parent home for most of my growing-up days.

My mom was an incredible single parent who worked extremely hard at her job, yet somehow never let things suffer around home. There were home-cooked meals and lots of love for my brother and me. But during this time, not a lot of my friends came from single-parent homes, and so I often felt like an oddball.

Because my mom was busy working full-time to put food on the table, and my brother — who inherited her hard-work ethic — also had a job from the time he was a teen, I was often home alone. And lonely. So I decided the best thing for me to do would be to throw myself into extracurricular activities and my studies at school.

I became obsessed with getting straight As. In fact, the only time I did not get an A in high school was during my freshman year when, just one semester, I got a B+ in Home Economics. I passed the cooking and cleaning sections with flying colors but couldn't seem to sew a straight line. When I graduated, I had a GPA of 3.979. The hundreds of hours spent studying and doing every lick of extra credit work in order to reach that goal was worth it to me.

I also joined each and any extracurricular activity that interested me: Spanish club, student council vice president, cheerleading captain, the school newspaper sports writer, softball, church youth group, National Honor Society, and on and on and on. I must have felt that filling my time with a flurry of activities would keep me from feeling sad about the fact that my parents were no longer married.

Across the street from our house was a little white country church. A new pastor had recently been appointed, and he had a wife and two darling children. One day, with everyone else at work and no meetings or practices for me, I was home alone. The pastor's wife, Pat, saw me out in my front yard throwing a softball up in the air to myself. She reached out to me, inviting me to play on the church's softball team. We struck up a fast friendship, and she soon became my mentor. She discussed with me something my mom had both mentioned and modeled to me — a relationship with God. I soon began my walk with him in earnest.

Pat noticed very quickly that I was filling my life with lots of activities. But instead of pointing this out in a negative manner, she always spoke words that were positive and encouraging. One afternoon she said to me, "I just know God has great plans for you. You love people, and you love God's Word. And you are good at writing and talking to people. I can't wait to see where life takes you as you sift through which activities you are meant to do. I believe in you."

I will never forget that conversation. During times when I doubted that I could ever become a speaker or writer, I replayed her words in my mind. And to this day she still encourages me. I have a team of about a dozen people who pray for me. Pat is one of those people. Now nearly in her seventies, she is still my biggest cheerleader. And her message to this often-insecure girl has remained the same: "I believe in you."

When I graduated high school and moved an hour away to attend a Christian college, I still liked to be involved in extracurricular activities, though not as many as I had done in high school. Dorm life kept me busy, and so for my outside-of-class endeavors I chose only drama, student government, and the college dance team. (I know that still sounds like a lot, but for me three activities represented a fraction of the activities I used to do!)

My freshman year during dance tryouts I was emotionally worked up and nervous. Being a member of the dance team was a pretty big deal at this school, bigger than the cheerleading squad I had been part of in high school. And so I thought I would give it a shot. I was anxious, with butterflies performing *Swan Lake* in my churning stomach, but I worked hard. When tryouts came, I did my very best and was hopeful I would get one of the eight spots on the team. As soon as tryouts wrapped up, we girls were all seated in a room and told that the results would be posted the next day in the school newsletter. I knew it was going to be one of the longest nights of my life.

As we gathered our things to wander back to our dorm rooms, however, the two advisers in charge of the dance team told me they wanted to speak with me for a moment. I wasn't sure if this was a good sign or an awful one.

They sat me down and gave me a very high compliment. They told me they were impressed with my dancing ability and with my creativity in making up dance routines. For being just a freshman they were pleased with my skill level. They then told me that I had made the team. My face beamed with joy. But hard on the heels of the compliments came the stinging, awful words. "However, we would like you to lose a little weight."

It was as if they had knocked the breath right out of my lungs. I couldn't speak. My face grew hot and red, and my palms began to sweat. They continued, "Even though you are probably one of the most skilled girls we've seen, we have to keep up a certain image. Therefore, we would like you to lose a little weight."

We would like you to lose a little weight. We would like you to lose a little weight.

Although that phrase was the one going through my head, it was not what my heart thought it heard. My heart thought it heard this: "We would like you ... *if* you would lose a little weight. If you don't? Then I guess we don't like you."

This led to all kinds of other thoughts that I imagined I heard and thought were true: *You aren't good enough. You've never been good enough. You are ugly. Undesirable. We are only going to tolerate you because you make up creative routines. If it weren't for that we wouldn't choose you for the squad. You. Are. Unloved.*

To say I was crushed would be an enormous understatement. Those words ringing in my ears sent me into a downward spiral of depression. I didn't eat anything for almost three days until my growling stomach forced me to. I probably dropped about ten pounds in those first couple of weeks.

Looking back at pictures now, I see one girl on the squad who was a bit heavier than I. I wonder if she got the same talk as I did? And there were two or three other girls who were about my same size. In fact, we used to trade clothing. I stared at the picture of that dance team, and the only thing I could determine was that my legs were a little flabbier than the others'. But I really wasn't any bigger. Did flabby legs warrant crushing a college girl's self-image?

Had I just been cut from the squad it would have stung for a while, but I would have gotten over it. I didn't continue in dance much past college. I wouldn't have cared that I wasn't considered a good dancer. But something as permanent as my appearance — when words were directed toward that, I felt I was labeled for all time.

Both of these phrases have echoed in the chambers of my soul over the years.

I believe in you.

We would like you to lose a little weight.

Each of these phrases would repeatedly return to the forefront of my mind throughout my adult life. At times when I was discouraged with my weight (or my performance as a mom or wife or friend), I would mentally beat myself up, ending my self-loathing rant with: *You. Are. Unloved.*

However, at other crucial junctures of my life, when facing an obstacle or a challenge I wasn't sure I was up for, my mentor Pat's words spoke loudly to my heart: *I believe in you.*

I think the two phrases my young ears — and heart — drank

in that day reflect this biblical truth, "Death and life are in the power of the tongue" (Proverbs 18:21 KJV). We can utter words that impart life, wholeness, and hope to others. Or our statements can kill — dashing dreams, crushing confidence, and dragging someone's spirit down.

Do you have any phrases from the past ricocheting in your mind or embedded in your heart? Were they uplifting or demoralizing? Words of life, or remarks of death? (Maybe you have both.) The fact that you can still recall these words days, months, or even years later should be a powerful reminder to be deliberate in carefully and prayerfully uttering your words — words that might be lodged in the hearer's heart for a long time. When voicing your opinion or making an observation to someone else, ask yourself, "Is my tongue speaking life or delivering death?"

Choose Your Words

Yes, the tongue has power. Words can hurt. Sting, destroy, devastate. Or words can heal, build up, encourage, and cheer. How are you going to wield your power? Here are some guidelines I hope will help you as you seek to use your words wisely, discerning what to say, how to say it, and when to say nothing at all.

1. Trade Places

Imagine you are hearing rather than speaking your words. How would you feel if what you are about to say were addressed to you? Ask God to remove from you any anger or impure motives that would taint your ability to really consider how it would affect you if the same words were spoken to you. If you struggle with having empathy for the person to whom you're speaking, maybe putting yourself in their place will help you to change your mind about what you are going to say or how you will say it.

2. Leave Some Things Unsaid

Can you get your point across without overexplaining? Do you really need to say *everything* that is on your mind? When the time comes to have an important talk with someone, spend some time thinking through the major and minor points you feel need to be covered. Then, cross some off. Boil it all down to the most important thing that needs to be said. This will keep you from droning on and on and increase the chances that your listeners will be responsive to what you have to say.

3. Temper Your Tone

When you were a teen, did your parents ever say, "Watch that tone of voice with me!"? What you were saying might not have been wrong, but the *way* you said it was. Maybe it was delivered with a sarcastic tone. Or an angry one. Or an accusatory one. My college roommate had a mom who didn't like the way she sometimes emphasized certain words that ended with the letter *T*. If her mother called her name from the other room, and my friend was particularly irritated that day, she would answer with a long and loud, "Whaaaattt?!?!", emphasizing the final *T* with a really harsh sound. Her mother, using her middle name for emphasis, would tell her to, "Watch that *T*!"

Especially when we have to say something difficult to someone, we need to do it with a tone of grace and kindness. It doesn't mean we lessen the seriousness of the words we are speaking. It just means we don't add to their harshness by the way we deliver them.

4. Consider Your Countenance

People don't just hear with their ears, they also listen with their eyes. The facial expressions people see as we deliver our words can also speak volumes. Of course, there are times when playfully talking to someone we know well, we may smile when we deliver a dreadful line, all in jest. But at other times we must be careful that what we say lines up with our countenance. Look the other person straight in the eye. Smile. Don't let your feelings come across too much on your face when they are talking. That can be distracting. Really listen with your whole being and focus with your eyes. Then, when it's time for you to talk, make sure that the countenance they see is attentive and open, not disengaged or critical.

5. Believe the Best Before Assuming the Worst

If you feel that you need to confront someone about something that affects you, it is best not to assume the worst about them. Believing the best before assuming the worst is the kind and honorable thing to do. Give them the benefit of the doubt. Don't jump to conclusions. Allow them to state their case before you make a judgment. Don't let your language be full of, "Well, isn't this just like you?" accusations, or "Once again you've done it" revisits of history. Which brings us to the next point.

6. Don't Get Historical

Fight the urge to rattle off every offense this person has ever committed against you. Sometimes the problem isn't that we are getting hysterical and losing our cool, but that we are dredging up the past and using it as a club to wallop the other person over the head. Treat each encounter as new without referring to the past unless there is a really good reason to do so. By starting with a fresh slate and administering grace, your conversation is less likely to escalate into something ugly, especially if you are discussing a conflict.

7. Be a History Changer

Just like famous presidents or my mentor Pat, you can change the course of history in the life of someone — or a lot of someones — you know. Think for just a moment about who in your life might be empowered with some history-changing words from you today. Do you know someone who's struggling? Someone who does not believe they are worthy? Someone who is his or her own worst enemy? Could you say or write these four powerful words to them today: "I believe in you"? Maybe you need to tell a friend she is a good mother, especially if she's in the midst of beating herself up over the poor choice her child just made. Or is there someone who needs to hear you say, "You're beautiful," just as they are staring into the mirror wishing they were someone else? Perhaps you know someone who would be so encouraged to hear that you trust their judgment, are amazed at their tenacity, are applauding their efforts, or admire their loyalty. Tell them.

8. Notice the One Who Least Expects to Be Noticed

When showering life-giving words on another human, don't just pick the people you know well. Notice the one who least expects to be noticed. The shy, single person at church. The faithful school janitor. The greeter at the department store. The single mom on the sidelines of the football field who just moved to your city after a nasty divorce. There is something deeply good about noticing a person who seems to blend in with their surroundings, not ever getting any attention. Jesus was always so in tune with those around him. He didn't just notice the prominent people. He noticed everyone. Even the less-than-lovely ones.

9. Choose Your Timing

Have you ever watched a stand-up comedian perform? It isn't always just the clever one-liners they deliver that make the people split their sides laughing. It is timing. A stellar comedian knows that good timing is everything.

The same is true when it comes to the words we deliver. Timing is everything. Be prayerful and careful about when you talk to someone, and I don't mean only when you need to have a hard conversation or lovingly confront. Even everyday discussions about family or workplace logistics can be initiated at the wrong time.

When calling someone, ask if they have a few minutes to spare or if you should set up a time later to connect. The best time to discuss even neutral matters with my husband is not at 9:45 p.m. at night. He needs to be up by 3:30 a.m. for work. And my family knows better than to try to chitchat with me when I'm watching a Detroit Tiger baseball game. It may be an important and long conversation you have to have with someone, or it might just require a few brief comments. Either way, watch your timing.

Ask God to give you a wise perspective: "A word fitly spoken *and in due season* is like apples of gold in settings of silver" (Proverbs 25:11 AMP, emphasis added). This verse suggests that merely speaking the right words isn't enough. We need to speak them in due season. I will admit I don't quite understand all of the "apples of gold in settings of silver" business. I tried scouring commentaries and Bible reference books to find out just what it means. No one seems quite sure. Perhaps just a lovely piece of art crafted from precious metals. In the right time and place, our carefully chosen words can impart beauty and value to the hearer. They can also prevent a misunderstanding that may damage a relationship.

Putting Principles into Action

I have struggled with rejection my entire life due to a few harsh words—hurling relatives and some past peer group situations.

(The saga of losing my social status in middle school at the beginning of this book was only one of many.) As a result, I realize I may be hypersensitive to situations in which I feel slighted, left out, ignored or, worse yet, unwanted altogether.

I had one of those experiences during the time I was writing this book. Try as I might, I couldn't shake the stinging feeling of rejection. I wanted to know why a decision had been made. I also wanted to make sure I wasn't reading things into the decision that really weren't there. I decided to pray about whether I should ask for a meeting with the person responsible for making the decision in order to get clarification.

Because I was in the process of really digging deep into the Scriptures for principles on how we should speak, I decided to apply as many of these principles as I could in hopes of a pleasant resolution to this situation. First I prayed about the timing of such a talk. I sensed God telling me to hold off for a while.

I promised myself I'd take my own advice and not bring up anything in the past when I spoke to this person. I also rehearsed the "Believe the best before you assume the worst" motto from my own Proverbs 31 Ministries and gave the other person the benefit of the doubt. Perhaps she had a reason I hadn't thought about for making the decision.

I listed out all the points I could make and questions I could pose. Then, I crossed out all that were not vital, determining to not bring up secondary issues.

Then one day while praying, pondering, and sipping herbal iced tea on my back deck, I sensed God saying the time was right. So I texted this person to ask for a meeting. When we met, though I was a bit nervous, my heart still slightly bruised, I made sure my countenance was pleasant. I respectfully relayed the events that occurred. I made sure to tell her what my perception was of the situation and resulting decision. Then I asked her if

I was reading it correctly? Had I misinterpreted? Or had I even done something wrong?

She quietly listened to me before she spoke. Then she explained and encouraged. Her explanation made sense. Her supportive speech cheered my heart. What could have been a relational disaster was averted because I took the Bible's advice when approaching this person. If I — in the flesh and without input from God's Word — had talked to others before talking to her; if I'd pouted to my friends and attempted to stir up some support on my side; if I'd spoken ill of this person, slinging mud as I did — we could have had ourselves a sticky and stressful situation. Instead, when it was over, I had answers. She had her reputation. And we both had peace and our relationship intact.

Are you facing a tough conversation with a friend, loved one, or coworker? Let God's Word guide. And lead. Let it soften and soothe. Choose to honor him with your words, and give others a chance to explain their actions to you.

In the Wake of Your Words

Over the course of the next few hours and days, you will be called upon many times to use your words. You will speak to those closest to you and likely also to complete strangers. What will be left after you have passed by? What will be left in the wake of your words?

I tried waterskiing once — and only once. It was the summer of 1976 and I was in the seventh grade. I had traveled with my mother and grandfather to upper Wisconsin for a week of vacation. My cousins were very skilled at all things aquatic. They were good swimmers. They loved to fish. And they could water-ski like no one's business. So they got the bright idea of teaching their land-loving cousin how to water-ski too.

Things started off well enough. I placed the skis on my feet and bobbed up and down in my bright-orange life jacket in the deep part of the lake, clutching the line attached to the boat my uncle Lee was about to drive. I had listened to all the instructions about how to get up on the skis and then how, once I was finally standing, to ski in a way that I would not fall.

My uncle revved up the engine and took off. I did everything I thought I was supposed to, and pretty soon I was standing up and skiing. However, I encountered a slight problem. My skis started to drift off course and into the wake, a V-shaped formation of rushing water generated behind a boat. While it is pretty, it is also powerful. And when a novice twelve-year-old water-skier accidentally gets her left ski caught in the wake, she soon gets the scare of her life.

I flipped. And flopped. I took in gallons of water in both my mouth and nose. And I continued to be dragged behind the boat in the wake of my uncle's joyride. Now, had I only been smart enough to let go of the line (double-duh!), this whole incident would not have been so traumatic. But I was in shock and wasn't thinking straight and somehow surmised that holding on for dear life was the right thing to do. As I said, it was the first and last time I ever went waterskiing.

Wakes are powerful. So are our words. And our word choices often leave behind a wake that can cause a ripple effect — for good or for ill — on all those around us. What is in your wake?

Grumpiness or grace?

Wrath or welcome?

Heartbreak or hope?

A fire hose of criticism or a gentle rain of healing water?

As we navigate through life's waters, may we be ever mindful of the way our words can impart life and love to those around us. I know you have it in you to be a woman whose words are as lovely as apples of gold in settings of silver. You can speak life. You can offer hope. You can be a history changer in the life of someone you know. How can I be so sure of this? It's simple.

Because I believe in you.

11

GOTTA HAVE
THE LAST WORD

Tips and Tricks
for Tempering the Tongue

To talk well and eloquently is a very great art,
but that an equally great one is to know the right moment to stop.

WOLFGANG AMADEUS MOZART

I know my daughter Kenna so well. Now that she is nearly a quarter-century old, she and I are more like close friends than mother and daughter. I am a work-at-home mom in Michigan. She is a cosmetologist who owns her own salon in North Carolina. Sometimes when we are yacking on the phone and I tell her a story about something that happened with a relative or friend, I anticipate what her response will be. If I had a nickel for every time I've said to her, "I just knew you'd say that!" well … I'd be a rich woman and no longer drive a rusty 2001 Ford Windstar van with 192,000 miles on it!

Even when we go shopping or out for a bite to eat when we are together, I have a pretty good sense of what she might comment on. She notices trendy hairstyles, makeup, and fashionable outfits — or those that are not (mostly those that are not!). She is a lover of healthy cuisine and fitness, the Bible and C. S. Lewis books. She is a photographer, so she has an eye for beauty in out-of-the-ordinary places and spaces. Because we have spent so much time together over the years, I have a keen intuition about how she thinks, what she might say, and how she will say it.

But however well I know my baby girl and her ways, it doesn't even come close to how well the Lord knows my thoughts and even my unspoken words. The psalmist declares that "before a word is on my tongue you, LORD, know it completely" (139:4). Not sort of know it. Not kinda have the gist of it. Not a pretty educated guess. He knows it *completely*! And I love how the Amplified Version of the Bible brings forth the richer meaning of the original Hebrew words of this psalm: "You sift and search out my path and my lying down, and You are acquainted with all my ways. For there is not a word in my tongue [still unuttered], but, behold, O Lord, You know it altogether. You have beset me *and* shut me in — behind and before, and You have laid Your hand upon me" (vv. 3–5).

Even though I know intellectually that God is always watching me, sometimes in the heat of life's squabbles and battles and mind-numbing demands, I forget. But if I really believe that what the psalmist wrote is true — God knows us, sees us, hears us — I need to make the last part of that verse my prayer: "Hem me in, Lord! Be behind me. Before me. Lay your hand upon me!" Or my loose translation: "Put your powerful hand over my big stinkin' mouth!" (Sorry that doesn't sound like a very spiritual prayer. It is, however, one of my very real and frequent ones!)

When I am mindful of the fact that God knows even my unformed words, it motivates me to speak only those words that will please him. And it also invites me to return the favor and get to know God better as well. I long to know his thoughts and his desires for me, to see and hear him clearly as he speaks to me through his Word. To get to know my Creator in a more intimate way, I must spend time with him exclusively. But I am busy. My life and schedule are full. Is being alone with God really that essential?

Time for a lesson from a teacup.

Retreat!

"I want honey in my tea. And a lemon slice too! Oh, and can I use great-grandma's teacup, pretty please? I'll be super careful. Pinky promise!", my then five-year-old daughter sweetly begged.

We were enjoying our afternoon mother-daughter ritual while her two baby brothers napped. Each day we pulled out china teacups and saucers from the collection in our old oak china hutch and slowly sipped herbal tea while I read a Laura Ingalls Wilder or Beatrix Potter book out loud to her.

This afternoon, however, she was asking permission to use an heirloom piece that had been passed down through four generations in my mother's family. While I knew my baby girl was grown up enough to be careful with the antique pink and white china cradled in her chubby little hands, something else made me deny her request. I tried explaining it to her.

"Sweetheart, I know you'll be careful, but we can't have hot tea in that cup. It has cracks. See?"

I showed her a few tiny, hairline fractures on the side near the handle. It wasn't cracked all the way through and could actually still hold water without leaking. However, if hot liquid were to be poured into it, the crack would give way, causing the petite cup to shatter. (Been there. Broke that!) There was just no way for the fractured piece to withstand the stress of a steaming beverage.

Our emotional lives are much the same. When we do not allow time to rest and regroup from the stresses of life, the resulting cracks in our spirit can leave us emotionally and spiritually fragile. We keep going at breakneck speeds, rarely slowing down long enough to be refreshed. And during these hurried and harried times our mouths are much more likely to be our enemy. Instead of forcing our family members to beat a hasty retreat from the onslaught of our verbal slings and arrows, *we* need to retreat: back away, slow down, chill out.

Even Jesus found it necessary to get away for a while. The disciple Mark wrote: "Then, because so many people were coming and going that they did not even have a chance to eat, [Jesus] said to them, 'Come with me by yourselves to a quiet place and get some rest'" (Mark 6:31). Jesus urged his disciples to get away to a quiet place. Being alone and quiet for a time would restore them and help to keep them whole.

When was the last time you spent time in a quiet place? No televisions blaring. No computers streaming webcasts. No iPods or MP3s cranking out music. If we never step back from the noise and demands of life, the stress of it all continues to chisel away at our souls, creating tiny cracks that could eventually cause us to shatter under the heat and pressures of everyday life — not to mention hurl harsh words at others in the process.

When we make time to respond to Jesus' invitation to go away with him to a quiet place, we can crack-proof our spirits, making them strong and rendering us ready to handle life. Even a few quiet moments spent with him can help mend cracks, renewing us and making us into vessels strong enough to be used by him. So are you willing to take time soon to slow down, get away, and rest? To find solitude in a hushed and holy place alone with our Savior, even if only for an hour or two? Here are some ways to do just that.

1. Get Up Early or Stay Up Late

I know it may sound simplistic, but it works. I do know at certain times in my life I needed every minute of sleep I could get: when I struggled with sickness or when I was the nursing mother of a newborn who woke up several times each night. But during the so-called "normal" times of my life, I find that forgoing fifteen to thirty minutes of sleep in order to appear before an audience of One is more than worth it.

2. Swap Spaces

If you want to be alone with the Lord for a longer stretch of time, consider finding a friend who has the same desire. And then? Trade places and spaces. You go to her house when she is not there and spend two or three hours alone in quiet. She will come to your house and do the same. Now, this works well if neither of you has any young children that need to be watched during the day. When I had little ones around my feet, here is what worked instead: I would watch my children — and the children of my friend — at her house while she went to my place for some quiet. The next week, we did the opposite. She corralled all of the kiddos and had a fun day with them at my house, while I went to her home for some quiet reflection. Going to the other person's house for your time alone is imperative. You are less likely to be distracted. When you try to do this at home, you spy the dirty dishes or know there is laundry to be folded or a junk drawer just screaming at you, "Organize me!" Removing these distractions allows you to clear your mind and center your soul on your time with God.

3. Find a Noisy Coffeehouse

It is a mystery to me but also a truth — somehow the clanking dishes and noisy espresso machines at a coffeehouse morph into white noise while I am sitting there reading and praying. I do not get distracted, and I actually find it fairly easy to focus in a busy coffeehouse. Not so much with one that isn't very busy. When there are long stretches of quiet and then just one person comes in the door, I get distracted by their conversation with the barista. But busy creates a buzz. The humming of the noise drowns out the distractions, and I am able to focus.

I know I am not technically alone — at least not physically — but somehow I am all alone in my thoughts. I feel able to concentrate. I not only can read the Bible, I can study it carefully. I can write prayers in a journal or spend time memorizing Bible verses. Yes, smack-dab in the center of the coffeehouse commotion!

4. Pretend It Is 1992

Or 1981. Or whatever year works for you. Just go back to a time when there weren't as many electronic distractions. I teasingly threaten my son and his friends that one day this summer I am going to declare it 1981 day at our house. No cell phones. If they want to communicate with someone they can use my landline. No cable TV. They may only watch the three major networks just like I did in 1981. No video games or iPod. I still have a trusty cassette tape player they may use, and they can always turn on the radio. (I'll give them three stations to listen to, like I had then.) And there was no such thing as a computer or laptop or iPad. Just beloved books. If they are arguing about Michael Jordan's basketball statistics, they can't "Google it" on one of their phones to prove each other wrong. (But I do have a nice set of encyclopedias they may use for research if they'd like.)

We need to time travel sometimes too. Unplug and unwind. Declare a fast from these modern electronic conveniences. Shut them down. Don't let them bleep or buzz. Just enjoy a day or a few hours in blissful, gadget-free quiet.

5. Check Out Local Retreat Centers

Just ten minutes from my home is a fabulous retreat center, owned by a particular denomination but open to anyone. It isn't anything fancy — just a large, brick-and-cinder-block building that looks much like a college dormitory from the 1960s. However, its lovely grounds are full of grape arbors, rolling hills and meadows, apple and peach orchards, and breathtaking perennial gardens. Benches and picnic tables are scattered about, inviting all who visit to sit and just be still. Inside the building are primitive yet pristine rooms for rent at $25 per night. Or if you just want to spend a day on the property, either outside or inside the building in one of the beautiful lounge areas, the library, or cafeteria, you may come from sunup till sundown for free. This retreat center has been a lifesaver for me that does not break our budget.

6. Split a Hotel Room with a Friend

What does it mean to split a hotel room with a friend? You arrange for an early check-in and late check-out. You will use the room from 1:00 p.m. when you check in until 9:00 that evening. Then your friend will join you for a sleepover. You'll enjoy some snacks and visit or catch some TV before turning in for the night. The next morning, you will get up at 6:00 a.m. and share breakfast in the hotel. Then you take off. Your friend now has the room until late checkout at 3:00 p.m. This way, you can each get an eight-hour span of time to be alone.

7. Go Outside to a Secret Spot

Sometimes it isn't always possible to get away for a whole or even a half day. Maybe all you have is a few minutes. If this is the case and weather permits, consider going outside. Create your own special or secret spot in your yard. At the back of our property we have a line of pine trees. Last summer I purchased a lovely stone bench and a freestanding, folding hammock at an end-of-season clearance sale. The stone bench sits in front of the line of pine trees, a serene place to sit and contemplate for a moment. Or I might take my Bible out with me to read a passage or two amidst the chirping birds and sounds of neighborhood children playing. The collapsible hammock is tucked away inside the patch of pines. Sometimes, during the day I will steal away for just ten or fifteen minutes and go lie on the hammock in the shade of the branches and pour my heart out to God. Just getting out in nature for a snapshot of time refreshes my spirit.

However you do it, once you get away and alone, how should you spend your time? What should you pray about? What is the best thing to do during retreat times to restore your soul? I find that even though reading the Bible or spending time in prayer or even reading a great classical book of the faith is just what I need, more often what I really need is a deadheading session with the Gardener of my soul.

Deadheading? What is that?

Faded Blooms

My mother-in-love is famous for her ability to grow the most beautiful things — tender and fragrant herbs that flavor her roasted potatoes or her lavender shortbread cookies; bright blooming annuals that display their splendor from May to September; flowering perennials that return year after year, poking their heads through the blackened earth revealing vibrant blossoms. She even staggers her plantings according to when they bloom in our Michigan climate to ensure that there will always be an array of color from the first hint of spring until fall.

I, too, although admittedly not possessing her knack for

nature, like to grow flowers and have tried my hand at an outdoor herb garden. However, it doesn't come naturally for me. I've had to read and study. And I have to schedule the required gardening chores just like an appointment: "Water herbs and flowers Mondays, Wednesdays, and Saturdays. Feed plants with Miracle-Gro on the first and fifteenth." But the most important task of growing these plants was the first lesson she taught me.

It's called deadheading.

Here is how it is done: As soon as any of those beautiful blooms begin to wither, fade, and turn brown, they need to be ruthlessly removed. So I search out every one and carefully pluck it off of its stem. It is a tedious, never-ending task. Just when I think I have removed every dried-up blossom, the next day a dozen more appear. It is important, however, to keep consistent.

When dead blooms are left clinging to the flowering plants, they sap the nutrition and strength from the core of the plant. They literally rob the plants of the energy they could be using to grow new and colorful blooms. The faded petals are, in a sense, dead weight that keeps the plant from looking its best. If properly plucked, however, the plant will consistently produce gorgeous and healthy blooms.

While plucking dead flower heads on my own patio this morning, I couldn't help but relate this chore to my life with God. I know full well that there are places of my heart, thoughts of my mind, and actions of my will that are nothing but dead weight to my spiritual life. The apostle James put it this way: "So get rid of all the filth and evil in your lives, and humbly accept the word God has planted in your hearts, for it has the power to save your souls" (James 1:21 NLT).

What does this mean?

Root out the ugly that threatens to choke and drain, and instead plant God's Word deep in our hearts. God's Word can save us from wrong choices, breakdowns in family relationships, and self-inflicted heartbreak. It can prevent our thoughts from turning into words that are detrimental to those around us and destructive to our own souls.

How about you? Could your heart use a good deadheading session? Are there faded blooms you have been carrying around that are sapping your spiritual energy and strength, causing heartache and tears? Get rid of the bad. Plant God's good Word in that spot instead. Then stand back — patiently now — and watch beautiful blooms begin to appear.

- When we admit our bitterness and ask God to replace it with a spirit of forgiveness, our love for others blooms.
- When we confess jealousy and ask God to help us to find contentment in him and the life he's chosen for us, our spirit settles.
- When we honestly acknowledge our anger and beg God to calm our rattled souls, we discover peace.
- When we stop talking about others behind their backs and fall on our faces conversing with God, we find a cleansing forgiveness that scrubs and then soothes our tarnished, tattered souls.
- When we stop finding fault with others and instead mind our own sin, we break down barriers that keep us from hearing from God.
- When we invite God to empower us to speak the truth in love — always seasoned with grace and saturated with respect and sprinkled with kindness — we heal broken relationships and strengthen others, preventing them too from snapping under the weight of uncomely words.
- Whenever we unearth any unclean thing in our hearts, we make room for God's Word to take root in its place as we invite the Holy Spirit to monitor our

mouths and help us avoid relational strife. We model to the watching world the forgiveness of God. In a sense, we live out loud the admonition of the apostle Paul to the church at Ephesus: "And do not grieve the Holy Spirit of God, with whom you were sealed for the day of redemption. Get rid of all bitterness, rage and anger, brawling and slander, along with every form of malice. Be kind and compassionate to one another, forgiving each other, just as in Christ God forgave you" (Ephesians 4:30–32).

Yes, intentional time alone and in stillness with God helps us to deal with any dead blooms of sin in our lives. And may I suggest one more action that has helped to prevent me from getting myself into a tangled web of verbal trouble in the first place? It is a subtle and simple visual reminder.

A Sign of Service

I remember begging my mom to get my ears pierced. I was in fifth grade and only one other girl in my class had hole-less lobes. I pleaded my case. "But Mooooooom! EVVVVV-ERY-ONE has their ears pierced but Heidi and me!"

I tried everything. My mom still said no. She told me that if God wanted me to have holes in my ears I would have been born that way. To which I replied, "Well, if God wanted me to have clothes on, then I guess I would have been born that way too. So tomorrow I am going to school naked!"

It didn't work.

My imploring was then bolstered by a Bible verse I presented to my mom that I'd heard a television preacher use. The loud man waving a big Bible had declared on the black-and-white screen right there in our living room the words of Psalm 40:6. His voice trembled like thunder, "Lord, you said it in your Word. You said it in your holy Word. You do not desire sacrifice and offering. But mine ear you have pierced!"

My mom didn't buy that either.

Finally, later that spring on my birthday — as she'd been planning to all along — my mama took me to Meijer Thrifty Acres (the midwestern version of Walmart) where, in the jewelry department, a nice lady wearing bright red lipstick and over-powering cheap perfume pierced my ears for me.

The pain was worth the cool.

In college, my friend Carmen got one ear double pierced. She said she did it to remind herself that she belonged to the Lord — that she was his slave.

You see, in the Old Testament, slavery wasn't always unjustly forced like the horrible reality of our modern world. It was more of an occupation: you were a servant with civil and religious rights. A slave worked for his master for six years and then had the option to leave. However, if he wanted to continue his ser-vanthood, he could; and as a symbol of his loyalty, his ear was pierced:

> But suppose the slave loves his wife and children so much that he won't leave without them. Then he must stand beside either the door or the doorpost at the place of worship, while his owner punches a small hole through one of his ears with a sharp metal rod. This makes him a slave for life. (Exodus 21:5–6 CEV)

I loved Carmen's idea of having a small hole in her ear as a sign of lifelong service to the Lord. An extra earring to remind her that she chose to serve God in all areas of her life. However,

I am a wimp. And the pain of the first ear piercing was enough for me!

But a few years ago, while shopping on lovely St. Simons Island just off the coast of Georgia where I was at a women's retreat, I had an idea. What if I wore a sterling silver toe ring as a sign of my service to the Lord? The women I was shopping with and I each bought one. (And I bought a thumb ring to wear in the winter instead of the toe ring, which pinches my toe when worn under shoes!)

I wear this toe ring every day to remind myself that I am a voluntary slave of Christ. And that I love my Master and the people he's given me to serve, like my family, church, neighbors, and others. When I see it, it reminds me that I'm not in control, God is. And it helps me realign my preferences with his when I want to be the boss of my life and my circumstances. When I grow weary of serving God selflessly, it's a simple reminder that I belong to him.

It also helps me to know that my Master is watching and observing how I interact with others as I use my words. Many a time I have bitten down on my tongue rather than toss out a string of cutting remarks because I spied my ring, right there on my left foot.

My toe ring also reminds me that my relationship with the Lord is for life. Yes, I am free to do as I'd like. There are no laws in my country against chucking my faith and running away. However, my toe ring reminds me: "Live as free people, but do not use your freedom as a cover-up for evil; live as God's slaves" (1 Peter 2:16).

Are you willing to commit to God with all your heart, mind, and soul? To serve rather than be served? To speak words of love and peace and truth rather than to use your words as weapons?

To carry out the wishes of your Master willingly and joyfully? Even though you are free, will you choose to be his slave today?

A pierced ear or toe ring is optional.

A Final and Flavorful Challenge

We've come to the end of our little journey about jargon. Our quest to learn to use our words properly: knowing what to say, how to say it, and when to say nothing at all. If our quest is successful, gracious speech will result. "Gracious words are a honeycomb, sweet to the soul and healing to the bones" (Proverbs 16:24).

I am sort of a Bible nerd. I love to not only learn the meaning behind the Hebrew or Greek words in Scripture, I also like to study certain English words that pop up at me, pogo-stick style, drilling down deep to understand why perhaps a particular word or phrase is used. And so, I grew curious one day: Why does God use a honeycomb to describe gracious, sweet, and healing speech? I didn't have to look far for my answer.

There is a teenage boy who lives in our neighborhood named Jake. He is an outstanding football player and wrestler. However, Jake is also a beekeeper who sells his jars of honey at local festivals and fairs. I decided to interview this high school entrepreneur one afternoon to discover all I could about the honey-making biz.

Jake told me that the flavor and intensity of honey depends on what kind of nectar the bees drink in. Clover nectar produces honey that is light and heavenly sweet. Another flower's nectar might create a dark, bitter product, with a lingering, unpleasant aftertaste. A smart beekeeper will be sure their beehive is strategically placed near a large patch of clover if they want to sell the sweetest, most delectable honey there is.

Jake also told me how crucial it is that the beehive also be placed in a location where the sun will hit it first thing in the morning, warming up the bees and causing them to get to work churning out the greatest quantity of sweet syrup possible.

"So," I questioned my young friend, "is it safe to say that the sweetness or bitterness of honey is determined by what the bee drinks in and the amount of time it spends in the sun?"

"Exactly!" he replied.

DING! DING! DING! We have a winner. I think I found my answer. Perhaps it is also true that the sweetness or bitterness of our words will be determined by what we drink in and the amount of time we spend with the Son. I pray that the journey you and I have taken together has given us both the tools to drink in what is good and the incentive to spend time with the Son each day so that we may speak words that are gracious, healing, and oh-so-sweet like honey. But we aren't finished yet!

Let's not let the progress we've made together over our time together just melt away like a double dip of tutti-frutti left out on the picnic table on a hot summer's day. Let's aspire to use our mouths with godly purpose.

To build ... not to break.

To bless ... not to badger.

To encourage ... not to embitter.

To praise ... not to pounce.

You with me? Good.

Now. A final challenge: Get away for a few minutes. Just you and the Lord. I want you to get out a nice note card or piece of stationery and write a letter to yourself. Yes. To yourself. In it, encourage yourself with what you have learned from this journey. What do you need to work on? Why do you need to work on it? What relationships are being damaged or precious time and memories lost because of how you interact with those in your life, whether they are family, friend, or even foe? Spend some time thinking about this and then let your pen and paper do the talking.

Write it out. Seal it up. Address it to yourself and affix a forever stamp to the front. Then give it to a trusted friend to keep. Have her pray about when she should pop it into the mail sometime in the next year without you knowing. When the letter arrives, open it and read your own words. I pray that you will have seen lasting progress in this important area.

Oh how I wish we were together face-to-face! As you turned the last page and closed this pink book, I would give you a hug and whisper my hopes to your heart.

I hope you don't let your mouth get you in as much trouble as mine has over the years.

I hope you will apply the biblical principles pointed out on these pages — the very ones that can restrain you from sinning with your speech.

I hope you speak life to others and impart courage to their souls.

I hope that when a family member's behavior threatens to knock the nice right out of you that you pause before you pounce.

I hope you make a habit — during the bumpy times of life — to hit your knees before you hit the phone (or tap away on the keyboard).

And I hope that long after this book has been placed on a shelf, passed on to a friend, or brought you a whole buck-fifty at your yard sale someday, that you'll still be reading The Book daily — God's go-to instruction manual for life.

Time for me to use my words one last time. This time as I have the privilege of praying for you.

Father, please bring to this sweet reader's memory
what we've learned together
in the pages of this book.
Help her to know what it means
to be angry but not sin.
To not let the sun go down while she still harbors
even a slight pinch in her heart toward anyone.
To be quick to listen, slow to speak,
and slow to become angry.
May she make it her aim to give a soft answer,
thereby helping to stop a family fight
before it even begins.
Enable her to be selfless and humble
rather than selfish and haughty.
May she zip her lips when she knows
she is beginning to gossip.
Empower her to avoid godless chatter
and instead speak only with a reverent purpose.
May her words not become a spark
that sets off a wildfire of regret.
Help her notice the one
who least expects to get noticed,
changing a life history with her encouraging words.
May she build up and not break down.
And most importantly, will you tap her on the heart
and remind her of the truth that you see everything, Father?

She so wants to please you.
Will you help her to do just that?
Assist her in keeping the lines of divine communication open.
May she continue to learn how and when
to keep her mouth shut
while she keeps her heart wide open toward you.
In Jesus' name, amen.

ACKNOWLEDGMENTS

To my Proverbs 31 Ministries sisters: I'm forever amazed at the ways God uses our team! I love serving him with all of you. Special thanks to Renee Swope, Glynnis Whitwer, Lisa Allen, Meredith Brock, Lynn Cowell, Lindsay Stafford, Amy Carroll, and Lisa Boyd for letting me bounce ideas off you. They always come back better than when I threw them.

To our Proverbs 31 Ministries president, Lysa TerKeurst. You are an astonishing leader and an even better friend. And I love how each of us are the "other mother" to our crazy kids. You have taught me so much about humbly serving, creatively crafting, generously sharing, and believing the best about someone before I assume the worst. Can't imagine life without you! (Although those 5:45 a.m. conference calls I could do without!)

To my agent, Esther Fedorkevich: You champion my projects and help me clarify God's direction. I'm so honored to be represented by the best in the industry and to have you as a friend too! I treasure our late-night processing and strategizing calls. Wait — no wonder I am so tired all the time. Can you and Lysa get in the same time zone, please, so I can sleep once in a while? ;-)

To Melissa Taylor: I have never in my life known someone who so effectively leads women in studying God's Word and also cares so deeply for them in the process! Your efforts have touched tens of thousands of women through Proverbs 31 Online Bible Studies. What a blast it was to have you be part of the DVD curriculum filming for this book!! (I still say we start our own P31 talk show!)

To my HarperCollins Christian family: Sandy Vander Zicht, Londa Alderink, Robin Phillips, John Raymond, and TJ Rathbun. Thank you for all you do to get my projects from scribbles on a legal pad to a book and DVD Bible study and into the hands of a woman who needs it. You all are so gifted and gracious.

To Lori Vanden Bosch: Thanks for perusing my words and helping to massage my message to make it the best it can be. And for leaving in a few more exclamation points this time. Ha!!!

To my 1,148 Go-To Gals, and also to the eight members of my personal prayer team: Your constant support, your creative ideas, and especially your powerful prayers keep me going and serving and recalculating when needed. Just. Thank. You.

To my "Soul Sisters" who — although usually only connected by our private Facebook page — are a key part of my life every day: Bloggers Courtney Joseph, Ruth Schwenk, Clare Smith, Darlene Schacht, Janelle Nehrenz, Joy Forney, Angela Perritt, Whitney Daugherty, Jen Thorn, and the event organizer extraordinaire Katina Miller. How I love our deep discussions about theology, marriage, parenting, and other such important matters such as Nutella pizza and how to properly fold undergarments. What wacky, off-topic hilarity often ensues. We could start our own comedy club!

To Candace Cameron Bure and Mandy Young: I so wish we could hang out more often. I love doing ministry with you both! What a team you are — a gorgeous and gregarious leg amputee and the *third place winner* from *Dancing with the Stars*! I smile just thinking about you two.

To Jill Savage, Heather Smith, Brenda Paccamonti, and the rest of the Hearts at Home gang: Wow! Over twenty years of encouraging moms together under Jill's confident and humble leadership. Thank you for letting me speak at your conferences. And for always having dark chocolate backstage! ;-)

To my prayer and accountability fab four who daily pound heaven's doors for my sake: Kim Cordes, Sharon Glasgow, Mary Steinke, and Lindsey Feldpausch. I. Can't. Even. (I'll just start to ugly cry if I do.) From the depths of my heart, thank you.

To my mom, Margaret Patterson: for your selfless love for me for nearly a half century. And for the creative celebrations you plan for the whole Patterson clan. You are the glue that holds our sitcom-like family together. (And the one who always brings an amazing vegetable tray.)

To my handsome college sweetheart and hubby, Todd: Almost thirty years, baby! You are so patient and prayerful. Thanks for your loyalty and faithfulness to God and to me.

To my three equally amazing and yet sometimes exasperat-ing kiddos (keepin' it real, folks): Kenna, Mitchell, and Spencer. I thank God every day that I get to be your mom. Never mind that I do it whilst also plucking the gray hairs from my head that result from your behavior sometimes. Thank you for loving me when I mess up as a mom, or embarrass you in front of your friends. (Sorry. It's just payback for that whole gray hair thing.)

To my Lord and Savior, Jesus Christ: For dying on the cross for my sins and then teaching me daily to die to myself. Indescribable.

MORE THINGS YOU CAN DO

Dear Reader:

For your convenience I've listed here the verses, self-assessment tools, and other relevant information from the book that I thought you might like to have handy in an effort to help you to know what to say, how to say it, and when to say nothing at all.

There is also a bonus recipe for Iced Honey-Lemon Poppy Seed Pound Cake and a cute gift tag featuring Proverbs 16:24: "Gracious words are a honeycomb, sweet to the soul and healing to the bones." Suggestions for photocopyable "Quips and Quotes" are presented as well. Enjoy!

From Chapter 4: Zip It and Pray

Top Ten Verses to Help You Watch Your Words

Here are ten fabulous verses to keep in mind — or to *cement* in mind by memorizing them — that can help you watch your words so they don't do damage to others, to yourself, or to God.

> Words from the mouth of the wise are gracious, but fools are consumed by their own lips. (Ecclesiastes 10:12)
>
> Whoever would love life and see good days must keep their tongue from evil and their lips from deceitful speech. (1 Peter 3:10)
>
> Those who consider themselves religious and yet do not keep a tight rein on their tongues deceive themselves, and their religion is worthless. (James 1:26)

May these words of my mouth and this meditation of
my heart be pleasing in your sight, LORD, my Rock
and my Redeemer. (Psalm 19:14)

Let your conversation be always full of grace, seasoned
with salt, so that you may know how to answer everyone. (Colossians 4:6)

Do not let your mouth lead you into sin. (Ecclesiastes 5:6)

Set a guard over my mouth, LORD; keep watch over the
door of my lips. (Psalm 141:3)

Do not let any unwholesome talk come out of your
mouths, but only what is helpful for building others
up according to their needs, that it may benefit those
who listen. (Ephesians 4:29)

Before a word is on my tongue, you, Lord, know it completely. (Psalm 139:4)

Though you probe my heart, though you examine me
at night and test me, you will find that I have planned
no evil; my mouth has not transgressed. (Psalm 17:3)

From Chapter 5: Motives and Manners

Here are a few questions to consider as you examine your
motives before you speak:

Am I certain what I want to say is true? If so, then perhaps you should say it. But before you do, consider the
remaining questions.

*Is my goal to have my comment help the person or situ-
ation at hand? Or is it to put a little pinch in their
heart?*

*Do I feel my words will bring a solution, or, if I'm totally
honest, might they cause more of a problem?*

*Even if what I plan to say is truthful, is my aim to say
something that will make me look better by comparison?*

Have I earned the right to speak to this particular person?
    If not, you should probably keep your lips zipped.
If I speak about this person to someone else, would I say
    the exact same thing if that person were sitting in front
    of me?
Are these words really necessary? Why?
Have I prayed about it, or only thought about it in an
    effort to plan what I've already determined to say?
Am I trying to play Holy Spirit and convict someone or
    guilt them into changing their mind?
If the roles were reversed, would I want the other person
    to say the same thing to me?

Once you have considered your blind spots and examined your motives carefully, then speak up if that is what the Lord is inviting you to do. For as Proverbs 16:23 says, "The hearts of the wise make their mouths prudent, and their lips promote instruction." Keeping your heart pure keeps your lips in line, and not only that — it makes what you *do* say instructive and helpful.

Proverbs' Top 10 "Tweets" on the Tongue

Here are ten great tongue-tempering "tweets" from Proverbs you can memorize, scribble on a sticky note, or use as a screen saver on your cell phone.

Don't let your mouth speak dishonestly, and don't let
    your lips talk deviously. (4:24 HCSB)
The wise store up knowledge, but the mouth of a fool
    invites ruin. (10:14)
Evildoers are trapped by their sinful talk, and so the
    innocent escape trouble. (12:13)
The Lord detests lying lips, but he delights in people
    who are trustworthy. (12:22)

Those who guard their lips preserve their lives, but those who speak rashly will come to ruin. (13:3)

The mouths of fools are their undoing, and their lips are a snare to their very lives. (18:7)

A gossip betrays a confidence; so avoid anyone who talks too much. (20:19)

Watch your tongue and keep your mouth shut, and you will stay out of trouble. (21:23 NLT)

A lying tongue hates those it hurts, and a flattering mouth works ruin. (26:28)

Do you see someone who speaks in haste? There is more hope for a fool than for them. (29:20)

From Chapter 7:
But I'm Just Sharing a Prayer Request

WHAT GOSSIP IS AND IS NOT

When we talk about the concept of gossip, does that mean we can't ever talk about another person when they are not present? I think the answer is no. It may sometimes be appropriate and necessary. So how do we differentiate between what is and is not gossip? Perhaps this checklist can help:

Gossip is when:

• We divulge a secret we were specifically asked not to share.

• We divulge a secret that we are pretty sure is not meant to be shared, even if we weren't explicitly instructed not to repeat it.

- We tell a story about someone we have not yet verified to be true.

- We speak about others in a way that paints them in a negative light so the listener will form an unflattering opinion.

- We talk in a cryptic way about someone, subtly suggesting something questionable or even scandalous about his or her character.

- We start out a story with a statement such as, "You know, they say ..." "They" can speak for themselves. Quoting "they" as the source of a story is a red flag. "They" are the origin point of ginormous amounts of gossip.

Gossip is not:

- Processing a conflict or difficult situation between you and another person (or persons) with a trusted and tight-lipped friend, family member, mentor, counselor, or support group. The words spoken are straightforward facts, and you make no effort to cast the other person in a bad light. You truly desire support, guidance, and prayer for handling the situation.

- Giving your honest opinion when asked about someone's character in a reference situation, such as when someone is applying for a job, a scholarship, or a leadership position.

- Giving your opinion about another person with words that impart grace, point out the honorable parts of their personality and character, and leave the less-than-lovely parts unsaid.

From Chapter 10: Something to Talk About

LOVE PROMPTS

Got a minute? Grab a pen! Use any of these prompts to get you started on jotting a note, an email, or a text to a loved one in your life. For some, the statement stands alone. For others, elaborate on the thought that is given. Your words are sure to bless your recipient!

Five Powerful Phrases to Speak to Your Spouse

I trust your judgment.
I'm glad I married you.
Here is what I appreciate most about you ...
I am with you.
Being your wife has taught me ...

Five Powerful Phrases to Speak to Your Child

You can do it.
A happy memory I have of when you were younger is ...
I am confident you can make good choices.
Being your mom has taught me ...
God has an amazing life planned for you.

Five Powerful Phrases to Speak to Your Parent

I'm not sure if I've ever told you before, but thank you for ...
A wonderful memory I have of my childhood is ...
I admire your strength.
How can I help you?
I am proud of you for ...

Five Powerful Phrases to Speak to Your Friend

My favorite thing about our friendship is ...
The best time I ever had with you was when ...
I am with you all the way.
The character quality I most admire in you is ...
You remind me of Jesus when you ...

A Sweet Treat to Accompany
Your Sweet Words

Here is a sweet and honey-themed food gift for you to bake. I've included a whimsical gift tag for you to photocopy on card stock, cut out, and include with your treat. Simply punch a hole in the tag and use some jute twine or thin curling ribbon to secure it around the foil-wrapped loaf or attach to a plate of sweet bread slices.

You might also like to give this tasty delight to someone along with a handwritten sentiment that uses your own sweet words. (Consider utilizing one of the Love Prompts listed in this section to get your words flowing.) You can bless a friend, relative, coworker, teacher, or even a stranger with a gift of honey-infused encouragement today!

Honey-Lemon Poppy Seed Bread

Ingredients

½ pound (2 sticks) unsalted butter, softened
2½ cups granulated sugar, divided
2 tablespoons honey
4 large eggs
¼ cup grated lemon zest
¾ cup freshly squeezed lemon juice, divided
¾ cup buttermilk
1 teaspoon pure almond extract
3 cups all-purpose flour
½ teaspoon baking powder
½ teaspoon baking soda
1 teaspoon salt
2 tablespoons poppy seeds

For the glaze

2 cups confectioners' sugar, sifted
3½ tablespoons freshly squeezed lemon juice
Dash of almond extract

Directions

Preheat oven to 350 degrees. Grease and flour two 8-inch loaf pans. With an electric mixer, cream the butter, 2 cups sugar, and honey in a large bowl until light and fluffy. Add the eggs, one at a time. Add lemon zest. Mix in ¼ cup lemon juice, the buttermilk, and almond extract.

Sift together the flour, baking powder, baking soda, and salt in a separate bowl. Combine the flour and buttermilk mixtures together mixing until smooth. Stir in poppy seeds. Divide the batter evenly between the pans, and bake for 45 minutes to 1 hour or until a cake tester comes out clean. If the top begins to brown too much, cover with a piece of foil gently set on top.

Combine ½ cup granulated sugar with ½ cup lemon juice in a small saucepan and cook over low heat until the sugar dissolves. Let loaves cool for 10 minutes. Remove from the pans and set them on wax paper or foil. Drizzle the lemon syrup over them. Let loaves cool completely.

For the glaze, combine the confectioners' sugar, lemon juice, and almond extract in a bowl, mixing with a wire whisk until smooth. Pour over the tops of the cakes and allow the glaze to drizzle down the sides.

For giving: Once the cake and icing have completely cooled and set, wrap in foil, being careful not to wrap the top and sides too tightly due to the icing. You may also give in bakery boxes designed for 9-inch loaf pans. You can find these at craft and gourmet food stores. You may also carefully slice the loaf and arrange some slices on a plate and cover with plastic wrap before giving. Whatever the presentation, be sure to include a copy of the tag featuring Proverbs 16:24 "Gracious words are a honeycomb, sweet to the soul and healing to the bones."

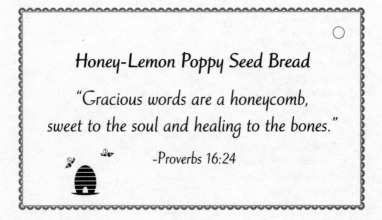

Honey-Lemon Poppy Seed Bread

*"Gracious words are a honeycomb,
sweet to the soul and healing to the bones."*

-Proverbs 16:24

MORE THINGS YOU CAN DO

Scripture Verses, Quips & Quotes

To help you remember some of the truth you have learned in *Keep It Shut*, photocopy any of the following Scriptures, quotes, or phrases on card stock. Then cut them out and place them where they are sure to be a reminder to you of how to use your words — or your silence — properly and in accordance with Scripture. Tape them to your bathroom mirror, prop them up at your kitchen sink, place them on your car's dashboard, or display them at your office desk.

Words are powerful and they
have consequences.

Don't say something
permanently painful just because
you are temporarily ticked off.

Advice From Proverbs:
"Don't Speak Too Much"
"Don't Speak Too Soon"
"Don't Speak Without First Listening"
"Don't Speak at All"

Hit your knees before you hit the phone
{or the keyboard}.

Make your speech laced with grace.

Prayer will make a man cease from sin, or sin will entice a man to cease from prayer. — John Bunyan

Believe the best before you assume the worst.

Sticks and stones may break my bones but words can never hurt me? No! Bruises fade and bones heal but a scorched heart may take years to mend.

Mind your own sin, sweetheart.

Are your words like a Snuggie®?

Don't be a Gasoline Queen!

Hang on a second, I gotta die.

The sweetness or bitterness of honey is determined by what the bee drinks in and the amount of time it spends in the sun. Likewise, the sweetness or bitterness of our words will be determined by what we drink in and the amount of time we spend with the Son.

"When there are many words, sin is unavoidable, but the one who controls his lips is wise." Proverbs 10:19

"In your anger do not sin: do not let the sun go down while you are still angry, and do not give the devil a foothold." Ephesians 4:26–27

"Be wise in the way you act toward outsiders; make the most of every opportunity. Let your conversation be always full of grace, seasoned with salt, so that you may know how to answer everyone." Colossians 4:5—6

"They have become filled with every kind of wickedness, evil, greed and depravity. They are full of envy, murder, strife, deceit and malice. They are gossips." Romans 1:29

"Before a word is on my tongue you, Lord, know it completely." Psalm 139:4

"Do you see a man who speaks too soon? There is more hope for a fool than for him." Proverbs 29:20

"The one who gives an answer before he listens — this is foolishness and disgrace for him." Proverbs 18:13 HCSB

"My dear brothers, take note of this: Everyone should be quick to listen, slow to speak and slow to become angry, because human anger does not produce the righteousness that God desires." James 1:19–20

"Even fools are thought wise if they keep silent, and discerning if they hold their tongues." Proverbs 17:28

"A soft answer turns away wrath, but a harsh word stirs up anger." Proverbs 15:1 ESV

"And do not grieve the Holy Spirit
of God, with whom you were sealed for
the day of redemption. Get rid of all
bitterness, rage and anger, brawling and
slander, along with every form
of malice. Be kind and compassionate
to one another, forgiving each other,
just as in Christ God forgave you."
Ephesians 4:30–32

"So get rid of all the filth and evil in your
lives, and humbly accept the word God
has planted in your hearts, for it has the
power to save your souls." James 1:21

"Gracious words are a honeycomb, sweet
to the soul and healing to the bones."
Proverbs 16:24

ABOUT KAREN

 Born in the middle of a March snow-storm in Michigan, Karen Ehman made her entrance into the world the same year as Lucky Charms, 8-track tapes, and the Ford Mustang. Her teachers said she had a love of writing but talked entirely too much. Today she still loves to talk — in books, online, and in person at her speaking events. Her favorite topic? Her Lord and Savior Jesus Christ, who she met at the age of sixteen on a crisp fall evening next to a roaring bonfire at a little country church retreat.

She has been described as profoundly practical, engagingly funny, and downright real. Her passion is to provide women with creative tools and doable ideas to help them live their priorities and love their lives.

Karen is a Proverbs 31 Ministries author and speaker, as well as their Professional Development Specialist. She also writes for their "Encouragement for Today" online devotions that bring God's peace, perspective, and purpose to over one million women daily. She has written seven books including *A Life That Says Welcome: Simple Ways to Open Your Heart and Home to Others, Everyday Confetti: Your Year-Round Guide for Celebrating Holidays and Special Occasions,* and the popular *LET. IT. GO: How to Stop Running the Show & Start Walking in Faith* which includes a companion DVD Bible study series.

She has been a guest on national television and radio programs including *The 700 Club, At Home Live, FamilyLife, Engaging Women, The Harvest Show, Moody Midday Connection,* and *Focus on the Family.* She is a graduate of Spring Arbor University and has been married for over a quarter-century to her college sweetheart Todd. Together they raise their three sometimes quarrelsome but mostly charming children in the boondocks of central Michigan ranging in age from teen to adult.

Though hopelessly craft-challenged with pitiful, partially finished scrapbooks, she enjoys antique hunting, herb gardening, and farm-market strolling, and has won several blue ribbon rosettes at the county fair for her cookies, cakes, pies, and breads. You'll often find her whipping up something tasty for her family and friends or the many teens that gather around her kitchen island processing life and enjoying something from Mama Karen's oven. (Although she only has three kiddos of her own, at last count at least seven teens had her in their cell phones as "Mom.")

You can connect with Karen through her website and blog: *www.karenehman.com* Twitter: Karen_Ehman

Facebook: Karen Ehman

Pinterest: karenehmanp31

Instagram: KarenEhman

Or at Proverbs 31 Ministries: *www.proverbs31.org*

To inquire about having Karen speak at your event, visit *http://proverbs31.org/speakers/inquire-about-our-speakers/* or call the Proverbs 31 Ministries Office at 877-P31-HOME

Proverbs 31
MINISTRIES

ABOUT PROVERBS 31 MINISTRIES

Karen Ehman is an author, speaker, and online devotion writer for Proverbs 31 Ministries, located in Charlotte, North Carolina.

If you were inspired by *Keep It Shut* and desire to deepen your own personal relationship with Jesus Christ, I encourage you to connect with Proverbs 31 Ministries.

We exist to be a trusted friend who will take you by the hand and walk by your side, leading you one step closer to the heart of God through:

- Free online daily devotions
- Online Bible studies
- Daily radio programs
- Books and resources

For more information about Proverbs 31 Ministries, visit: www.Proverbs31.org.

To inquire about having Karen speak at your event, visit www.Proverbs31.org and click on "speakers."

Let. It. Go.

How to Stop Running the Show and Start Walking in Faith

Karen Ehman

Doable ideas, thought patterns, and tools to help you LET GO OF YOUR NEED TO CONTROL

The housework. The meals. The kids. Many women are wired to control. But trying to control everything can be exhausting, and it can also cause friction with your friends and family.

This humorous, yet thought-provoking book guides you as you discover the freedom and reward of living a life "out of control," in which you allow God to be seated in the rightful place in your life. Armed with relevant biblical and current examples (both to emulate and to avoid), doable ideas, new thought patterns, and practical tools to implement, *Let. It. Go.* will gently lead you out of the land of over control into a place of quiet trust.

A companion video-based study for small groups is also available.

Let. It. Go.: A DVD Study

How to Stop Running the Show and Start Walking in Faith

Karen Ehman

God Called. He'd Like His Job Back.

Most women are wired to control life's details. In this humorous, yet thought provoking six-session, video-based study, Karen Ehman guides you to discover for yourself the freedom and reward of an "out of control" life. Armed with relevant biblical and current examples, new thought patterns, and practical tools to implement, *Let. It. Go.* will enable you to control what you should, trust God with what you can't, and most importantly, decide which one is which.

Sessions include:
- God Called and He'd Like His Job Back
- Combating the "Me First" Mentality
- Pursuing the Appearance of Perfection
- Practicing the Art of Soul Control
- When Comparisons Lead to Over-Control
- Fixing Your Eyes on the Attitude Indicator

Available in stores and online!

ZONDERVAN®
.com